The Winning Mindset

An Introduction to Paraconscious Programming (PP)

What people are saying about PP:

"For me Martyn has been the missing link .... I didn't always focus in ways that best served me. I do now!........ I've since continued to grow and mature as a bowler and person with Martyn's input. He's a canny lad. For me this season has got better and better. Martyn has taught me the tools to continually be the best that I can be. Cheers Big Lad!"
Yorkshire and England A Fast bowler, Steve Kirby

"For my players to wait around for up to three hours after training to talk to you is extraordinary. You have something very special there, Martyn"
FA Cup winning former West Brom, Wimbledon and Wales football manager Bobby Gould

"My experience of sports psychologists was that they stated the obvious and pointed out the problem. Nothing changed. Or they tried to change what I liked about myself which just brought up my resistance. The strength of Martyn's approach is that it helps me drop my resistance to the positive changes that I know will help me. It sometimes seems bizarre or radical but what is important is .... IT WORKS! This PP stuff creates results. Changes occur. You get solutions. If you want to be the best you can be (and why wouldn't you?) then this work is astonishingly powerful, try it."
Second team and U-19 coach, Leicestershire County Cricket Club, Lloyd Tennant

"When I was riding I always knew that self belief and a positive mindset was essential. Martyn's book will help you to achieve this outlook and I believe the tools he has developed can help you to realise your potential, not only in sport but every area of your life."
Peter Scudamore - 8 times Champion Jockey, TV Personality and one of the greatest sportsmen of our times.

"After being released from my county contract the future looked bleak. A lot of negative emotions surfaced that I didn't know how to deal with. Martyn taught me his PP Method and I was quickly able to refocus myself and drop negativity. Sure it came and went to start with and I'd ring him for a few reminders but every part of my life started to get better. I rediscovered my motivation and enjoyed a brilliant summer. My keeping has been top quality and I have played all around the country scoring hundreds (some big hundreds) everywhere I've played. My approach is more relaxed, more positive, I am definitely more mature, and I'm loving my cricket ..... without Martyn's help it could have been all too different."

Wicket keeper and batsman, Gloucestershire County Cricket Club, Steve Adshead

"I had stopped enjoying my football. I was constantly stressing about whether I'd play and whether I'd score. It was putting a strain on at home. I'm not sure what you did Martyn but I feel so much better, like a weight's been lifted. I'm enjoying it again, I feel I'm playing better and my wife's pretty chuffed too."

Crewe, Port Vale and Cheltenham Town footballer, Tony Naylor

".... his easy and friendly style makes it easy to work on personal issues - rare with psychologists.... I became more relaxed before and whilst at the crease. Martyn helped my self-belief. I also became more confident about hitting the pitch harder when bowling"

England U19 and Sussex County Cricket Club all-rounder, Luke Wright

"A major benefit was, I now think about what I want to do rather than what I do not want to do. This has also rubbed off on my team mates"

Harry Gurney, Leicestershire County Cricket Club U-16/17s

"One of my biggest fears is looking an idiot in the field, probably more so than inadequate with the bat, when in the first team. Having read through the first 30 or so pages of the book I felt relaxed and ready to play, didn't even feel as though I needed to deal with the negatives 'cos I didn't have any. Not a feeling I've experienced much. Anyway I was left out of the side but fielded the whole game as Darren Maddy was injured. I was the best fielder on the park so much so that Daffy (Phil Defreitas) as well as the two coaches and even John Embury, when shaking my hand after the game, commented on my excellent fielding! I don't know where it came from, I was brilliant."

Damian Brandy, all-rounder Leicestershire CCC

"Martyn helped me clean some deep seated resentment out of my subconscious, which enabled me to refocus on what I wanted for myself rather than focusing on the negative. It meant that my performance level immediately returned. I had come to be playing well below my best. One short session and I returned to my best form."

Michael Duff, Cheltenham Town and Burnley defender

"Well, it's been amazing really. My confidence at the crease has meant that I'm enjoying my best form for some time. The things that used to play on my mind - just don't. My fielding has never been my strong point, in fact last season I had a shocker at gully. As captain it's really important to lead by example and I've already held some pretty good gully catches since working with Martyn. It's funny really 'cos it's even helping my wife's tennis."

Guy Home, Captain Shropshire County Cricket Club

"I saw lots of psychologists and other experts when I was trying to overcome the yips and nobody was able to match the practical help that I received from Martyn. He taught me how to escape the trap of self-denial that I'd fallen into.
In short he helped me turn my game around and actually to allow

myself to enjoy playing cricket again. He not only helped me overcome my problems with bowling, but he set me on a path of positive development both as a cricketer and as a person."
Gavin Hamilton, England and Durham County Cricket Club

"Being able to release all thoughts of what you don't want to happen, being relaxed and having clarity of intention at speeds that make your mind fearful will always make you a safer and better slier. Whether you ski for fun or professionally, these tools that Martyn has developed will help you be the best you can be. In 21 years of teaching I've seen nothing more powerful to help quieten the mind and grow your courage."
Alan Muir, B.A.S.I. II Ski Teacher,
member International Ski Instructor's Association

Author, self belief guru, life coach, human behaviourist and a leader in the field of performance psychology, Martyn Court works with some of the top performers, players, coaches and managers in the world of sports, also those who wish to improve their performance and achievement in any area of their life.

His speciality is the subconscious mind and helping people to use it's power to achieve success and results beyond what they consciously thought was possible.

Over the last five years he has been developing Paraconscious Programming™ through his work with leading sports performers. It is a unique method for growing self belief and mental strength.

His style is sometimes painfully direct, often wickedly humourous but **always** he is passionate about helping anyone become the best that they can be. He says," We just may be bottomless! We may never be able to reach the point beyond which we can't improve. Certainly it can be a lot of fun exploring!"

First published in 2003 by

Sidney Publishing Group,
Star Time House,
8 Albert Place,
Cheltenham. GL52 2HW

e-mail: success@martyncourt.co.uk

To order or view other titles on-line:

www.martyncourt.co.uk

Printed in Victoria, BC, Canada

Note for Librarians: a cataloguing record for this book that includes Dewey Decimal
Classification and US Library of Congress numbers is available from the Library
and Archives of Canada. The complete cataloguing record can be obtained from
their online database at:
www.collectionscanada.ca/amicus/index-e.html
ISBN 1-4120-2966-X

TRAFFORD

This book was published on-demand in cooperation with Trafford Publishing.
On-demand publishing is a unique process and service of making a book available
for retail sale to the public taking advantage of on-demand manufacturing and
Internet marketing. On-demand publishing includes promotions, retail sales,
manufacturing, order fulfilment, accounting and collecting royalties on behalf of
the author.

Offices in Canada, USA, UK, Ireland, and Spain
book sales for North America and international:
Trafford Publishing, 6E–2333 Government St.
Victoria, BC V8T 4P4 CANADA
phone 250 383 6864   toll-free 1 888 232 4444
fax 250 383 6804   email to orders@trafford.com

book sales in Europe:
Trafford Publishing (UK) Ltd., Enterprise House, Wistaston Road Business Centre
Crewe, Cheshire CW2 7RP UNITED KINGDOM
phone 01270 251 396   local rate 0845 230 9601
facsimile 01270 254 983   orders.uk@trafford.com
order online at:
www.trafford.com/robots/04-0794.html

10   9   8   7   6   5   4   3   2

I dedicate this book to Lester and Hale, words cannot express my respect and gratitude. Without knowing you I would not have seen the possibilities.

Acknowledgments

In many ways I feel that others have contributed to this work as much as I have. I thank you all, mentioned or not, from the depth of my heart.

I particularly am grateful to **Lloyd Tennant**. It's been a pleasure learning from you, I applaud your openness to what may have seemed scary concepts.

I am lucky to have everyone at **Spa PR**, Cheltenham on my team, thanks Lyndsay.

Steve Kirby 'ay up big lad!' I feel that I have learnt as much as I've taught. You are awesome. A massive England career for you is assured if you just keep doing the right things. It's been a pleasure knowing you.

One of the stars of my team is **Tom Wakefield** at **furryfeetstudios.com**, cheers Tom.

Colin turner for his photographs and the **Gloucestershire Echo** for theirs, thankyou.

Sheddy, go boy! You know you have all it takes, you're a star, I have loved working with you.

David Lloyd, Paul Allott, Ian Botham, Gavin Larson and **Peter Scudamore** for granting me interviews.

Gavin Hamilton for having the desire to go again. You will get all you deserve mate!

Nikki, the challenges you set me have made me so much stronger than I have ever been. I thank you deeply.

I am very fortunate to have stumbled across the **Hotel Alexandra** in **Lyme Regis**. The setting and welcome extended to me made completing this project a joy. I wish to publicly thank all the staff that made my working breaks there perfect. If this book is any good it is in large measure to your being very good at what you do. Thank you all. Especially thank you to Nicky and David your artistry with food kept me buoyant. RESPECT!

Someone said, "Good food is the fuel of the writing classes." It might have been me! I highly recommend a visit. E-mail: alexandra@lymeregis.co.uk

My children have taught me so much. I love you for being who you are and the way you are. Fay, Niall, Luke and Jordan thank you for the unique joy that only you each bring. I must have done something wonderful in a previous life to deserve you guys.

Finally, to my parents for giving me this chance and to everyone I've ever met, and those I've not, who have in some way impacted on my life, seemingly good or bad, you've helped make me what I am and I'm happy about that. Thankyou.

The Winning Mindset

(Through Paraconscious Programming™)

Martyn Court

"Without the right thoughts, the courage, the confidence, you can have all the talent in the world and it counts for nothing."

Sir Vivian Richards

Contents

1 Introduction

"So little is required to be successful in sport. It's certainly most-ly a matter of psychology, and in the end it's that psychological difference that decides whether you win or lose." -
Sven-Goran Erikson

Paraconscious Programming™ is one of the most powerful methods known to man of enhancing performance. Some sports performers only turn to a mind coach when things are going wrong. Others, like Tiger Woods, see psychology as a vital skill. With this unique and leading edge method (Paraconscious Programming™) Martyn Court has enabled top performers to go beyond what they had previously thought possible.

How can you go beyond what you think is possible?

Until May 6th 1954 the mass consciousness stated that no man could run a mile under 4 minutes. Man simply wasn't built that way - it was physically impossible!

One man wouldn't accept the limit and hatched a plan to achieve the seemingly impossible. Once Roger Bannister changed the mass consciousness, some 50 plus athletes also ran sub 4 minute miles in the next 6 months.

Most people haven't the courage to challenge 'accepted wis-dom' or the mass consciousness and so settle for blaming something, anything, for their lack of success. Alternatively they take an arrogant, closed minded stance saying *"but I'm already too good"* or *"well, I never really wanted that"* or some-thing similar. This may satisfy the ego-mind or conscious mind but if deep in your heart or subconscious mind there lies that nagging feeling - **'but what if I could be better?'** Then ask yourself: How committed are YOU to YOUR suc-cess?

I am sure Tiger Woods never has the thought - I am good enough. He just enjoys exploring how good he could be.

How good could you be?

With Paraconscious Programming™ YOU TOO can go beyond your conscious boundaries and achieve the seemingly impossible.

So what is Paraconscious Programming™?

Many people think that something needs to be wrong before they would use a performance psychologist. Yet these psychological performance enhancement tools can simply take you from where you are now (however good that may seem) to where you want to be - even if that seems impossible - FAST!!!

We all know we have a conscious mind, and indeed a subconscious mind. Yet how many of us know how the subconscious mind works and how it can hold you back from having what you want or performing at the top of your ability?

Certainly few people have mastered the subconscious but what of the third level of consciousness? This is little known, yet central to the phenomenon called 'The Zone'.

The PP Method consists of proven yet extraordinary tools that, once learned AND USED lead to performers being able to put themselves into the 'zone of optimum performance' at will. Martyn Court's ability as a mind coach is renowned around the world. It can seem beyond belief the way he intuitively uncovers deeply embedded subconscious blocks that hold performers back from levels of performance and achievement and enables them to attain levels they may not have thought possible themselves.

2 Competitiveness - a two edged sword

"It is not the mountain that we conquer, but ourselves."
- **Sir Edmund Hillary, conqueror of Mount Everest**

We live this life on a plane of duality or polarities (you can't have in without out, you can't have up without down etc.) this makes life both challenging and amusing. These paradoxes can either entertain us or frustrate us, it is simply a case of how we choose to perceive them. The key is to understand that we do live in a world of duality. It is inescapable; you can't have good without bad , you can't have winning without losing, you can't have hot without cold, you can't have excitement without fear etc.

Even, you can't have matter without antimatter.

However, we try to operate and live our lives as though we can change that. We give ourselves trouble when we try. What we can do, is change how we perceive these facts. Courageous people do not have an absence of fear, they simply honour their fears (fears have a use - they can keep you safe) and move on beyond them positively. People acting courageously simply acknowledge the warning that any particular fear has to impart. Then they gather their courage, step out of their comfort zone and go ahead and achieve their desires ANYWAY.

Competitiveness likewise has a positive and a negative side. Competition in the marketplace can give customers better choice, however it can also make providers of a service or product cut corners and reduce quality in order to compete.

So it is in team sports. Competitiveness can be a two edged sword.

Using this natural part of us (our competitive/aggressive

tendency) as a constructive means of motivating ourselves to grow and improve and to be the best we can be, can only be good. Often, however we see the dark side of competition being displayed. This can manifest as simply being a bad loser, cheating, turning on team-mates etc. and in extreme cases as in recent premiership football matches outrageous acts of provocation, verbal or physical abuse and demeaning behaviour such as spitting and even physical violence.

Focusing competitiveness constructively

Clearly, how you focus this natural and awesome power is critical. If you focus it on the opposition then that is better than focusing it on your team mates. However, this puts you into a one up one down mentality. Your mood swings will be dictated by the opposition. If they are worse than you and you perform well then you'll feel good. If, on the other hand, they are better than you, you may feel defeated and deflated. This could take your mind off what you are trying to achieve and certainly will not help you stay relaxed and focused. People who think this way fall prey to 'big fish - small pond' syndrome. They effectively choose their opposition, where they can, to ensure feeling good about their results and their performances.

This is obviously a downward spiral. They play against weaker opponents, they therefore don't have to stretch themselves, their own performance levels drop. Conversely, WINNERS, instead of avoiding the pain associated with poor performance and defeat, USE it to motivate and challenge themselves. They know that the fun of a positive competitive nature is that they will constantly enjoy pushing their own boundaries and levels of performance. This is the most constructive use of what is essentially a survival instinct.

Years ago someone I knew used to deride me. *"You are so*

competitive" they would say. Then I used to deny it (although I probably WAS over competitive). Now, however, I am glad for it. Without that desire to extend myself I wouldn't have the motivation to finish this book, to keep myself fit, learn new and exciting things. In short - be me!

Very often people who deride others as competitive are simply not acknowledging their own competitive nature but becoming defeatist as a defence mechanism. Sadly a very destructive focus for their competitive instinct. They are reduced to sniping from the sidelines to make themselves feel better - what the Chinese call 'cutting others heads off to make yourself feel taller'. The reality of this approach is that on a subtle subconscious level it DOESN'T make you feel better. You simply despise yourself for being so destructive. Your self esteem falls. How can you then go out and perform and earn success for yourself, when on a deeper level you don't actually admire and respect yourself?

I have seen this in business frequently. A really focused person, very driven, climbs all over others to succeed. Yet when the sought after success arrives the victory seems so hollow, there is little joy in the victory.

Every one (except the ref.) saw the 'hand of God' incident. Maradonna deliberately cheated on the world's greatest stage for his sport, in order to win. What was he thinking? He was the greatest player, by general consent, in the world game prior to that decision. Afterwards his life became meaningless, his football and entire life began to fall apart like the rotten morals and values that lead him to decide to cheat. The success and respect that he so cherished were not achieved. Now instead of achieving immortality through his incredible talent he has achieved infamy for his outrageous action. Instead of achieving respect he has achieved condemnation for trying to justify his wrong doing.

The only mature and sane response is to have compassion

for him and gratitude for the lesson that he has given us. Oh and to LEARN that lesson!

Correct focus for your competitive instinct

To conclude, then, it simply doesn't serve you to do anything other than hold the value in mind of wishing to enjoy the challenge of seeing how good YOU can be. Not in comparison with anyone else but just how GOOD you can be. You are competing with yourself in order to be the best you can be. This way you view competition with anyone else as simply marking your card. The negative pressure then that some people put on themselves won't exist for you. You will only be grateful for opponents, as they provide you with a means to measure your progress on your enjoyable journey to how good you can be. It is important here to understand that all pressure IS SELF IMPOSED. A six foot putt is a six foot putt whether it is on the practice green or to win an Open. Whether it is the last practice putt before breakfast or whether a £million rides on it. The pressure is in your mind, YOU create it. If you think this is wrong you are suffering from a victim mentality. Learn to take responsibility for your own life. It will change you for the better. I shall deal with this in Chapter 6 - Single Pointed Focus

So let's take our competitive nature and apply it. Let's set it to work now in growing our self belief - without which you'll never win anything or become good at anything except by accident!

3 Self Belief - The key to fulfilling potential

"First confidence, then form." - **David Gower**

Everyone can benefit from growing their self belief but how do you go about it? For many their self belief comes from external conditioning. It is true that being encouraged will lead to greater confidence. This leads to engaging in activities wholeheartedly and increases the likelihood of success. Repeated success leads to enhanced self belief. However, for some this self belief is a fragile commodity because it has been built by others. The danger is that if it is built up by others it may also be taken away by others. This subconscious insecurity could become a problem at some point especially under extreme pressure.

Denial of doubt

It is quite common to come across people who are trying to build their self belief by denying that they have any doubt. This is often observed as 'puffing' or 'crowing' and always looks like arrogance rather than very high levels of confidence or belief. The problem with denial is it is self defeating. If someone is not open to the possibility that they can improve (arrogance) then they will get to be right! No one can help them and they can't help themselves either. Much like an alcoholic that says " I don't have a drink problem" no one can help them change. So too with sports performers who deny their self doubt, they will never really be able to build unshakeable and massively high levels of self belief.

Here in Britain we have, very commonly, a misunderstanding of these issues. We often look at confidence and misinterpret it as arrogance. It is often said of the Australian cricket team that they are arrogant. They are not. They have, to a man, very high levels of self belief. Conversely, many of our top English players in trying to look confident become (inadvertently, I'm sure) arrogant. Arrogance is a closed minded state. The feeling of I'm already good enough, you can't teach me anything etc. Now for a while, this may serve as a form of confidence. A good friend of mine, Lloyd, is a top cricket coach. He speaks straight. He calls it 'bullshit confidence'. He's right. It's a weakness. You see, consciously you are massaging your own confidence with this defence mechanism - " I'm already good enough". Yet deep down on a subconscious level you doubt your ability.

Why would you need to pretend otherwise? AND IF YOU'RE NOT PRETENDING .... why not be open to the possibility that you could improve?

In the extreme this takes the form of delusion. I have recently experienced a raft of young professional players, all with talent, both in football and cricket, who have been released from their contracts. The reason - delusion. They belligerently would not look at their weaknesses. They insisted that they were better than everybody else thought, to anyone who would listen. Yet their performances consistently failed to live up to the levels they claimed. They failed to walk their talk. ACTIONS always speak louder than words. The world is full of failed potential.

Self awareness

So a key to gaining self belief is having a highly honed sense of awareness.

How do you grow your awareness?

Well everyday, every moment, presents you with opportunity. The first essential is to relax.

Very few people do what they know makes sense. We know that being relaxed, yet highly aware, and focused is the only way you will ever achieve the best results that you seek. Yet, knowing it seems to be enough for many - we rarely do it. However, like buying a mower and hanging it in the shed is not what keeps your lawn looking lovely. So too having this knowledge is not enough. USING IT is what makes the difference - what gives you the desired result. With sports performance the temptation is to 'try hard', yet less efforting and more effectiving is what successful people do. So stop trying hard, relax into being effective.

So treat yourself. Next time you need to pop to the shop use it as an exercise in growing your awareness. Take your time don't rush there. Engage all of your senses. Don't write a list. Trust yourself. Know how many items you are going for and know that you have time to stand and remember what they are. Then ENGAGE ALL OF YOUR SENSES. As you walk slowly out of the house. Actually HEAR what's going on.

Allow all the noises, rhythms and sounds to enter your consciousness, don't judge it as good or bad, don't express an opinion as to whether you like it or not. Just witness it objectively, i.e. without judging. Allow VISION to expand. Instead of looking where you are going and rushing there as you usually do, DON'T LOOK WHERE YOU'RE GOING. Look everywhere else. See what others see and you usually miss. Drop your preconceived ideas about what things are and see them for the first time the way they really are! If something catches your eye, stop and really observe it. Allow yourself to appreciate it. We pigeon hole for expediency but it means we don't SEE the reality before our very eyes. In ball games this can lead to effectively guessing where the ball is going rather than watching it right onto your racket, bat, foot or into your hand.

Engage your other senses too. SMELL everything that exists. Just allow all fragrances, good or bad to come into your awareness. Again don't allow your rational mind to qualify or judge. Just allow yourself to witness what your senses are sensing. Your awareness is expanding as you do. And now finally FEEL everything that you can feel. Feel the ground under your feet can you feel unevenness? Can you feel the joints in the paving, the inside of you shoes, your socks, your clothes against your body, the air against your skin? This exercise is for you to enrich your experience but more to train you to expand and grow your awareness. THIS WILL REAP YOU BENEFITS, LATER, THAT YOU MAY NOT BELIEVE POSSIBLE NOW .... DON'T BELIEVE ME. TEST IT OUT FOR YOURSELF .... YOU DESERVE THE BENEFITS THIS WILL BRING!

When we are stressed we are easily irritated and we are intolerant so we block out most of what is going on. Our awareness therefore shrinks back. We are subconsciously sanitising life. We make our life safe (dull and grey) through our perception, we limit our view of the world to fit what we think we can cope with in our stressed state. Sadly our perception of life becomes drab and depressing. In effect a self fulfilling prophecy. Yet obviously NOT very fulfilling! It is unfulfilling so we look for stimulation through artificial means. Very often destructive ones.

So step out of your usual routine. Get out of the rut.

Rut-hopping

I run seminars in which I help people live life more fully, a more expanded version of who they have been up to then. Increasing awareness is a key tool and I use exercises that I call 'rut-hopping' to help them achieve their ideal life.

You too can use this technique. If you have a partner you may invite them to join you. But I don't advise coercing them. Simply try your best to do as much as you can differ-ently from the way you normally would. Drive a different route to work, wake at a different time, dress using a different routine or order of doing it. Physically, in your training or preparation you will already be doing this. Ski instructors will make sure that you start exercises on a different ski or leg. Physical fitness routines are designed to balance the building of strength. Yet mentally we often allow ourselves to become limited to a set routine, a set way or even to a heavily limiting preference: being one footed as a footballer or one handed as a fielder in cricket for example.

Tennis players simply don't rule out backhand shots or forehand shots just because it doesn't seem natural or it's their weak side. Top footballers like Zidane and Ronaldo have worked on their skill level such that they will use whichever foot is the more appropriate in order to be the best they can be. Jonty Rhodes could pick up and throw with either arm. Jonny Wilkinson can drop a goal off either foot and has benefited by scoring points when a one footed kicker would have been charged down. I am sure there are other examples of people who have not allowed themselves to become limited by what is after all merely a personal preference.

I listened to Ian Ward being interviewed. He was given his chance to open the batting for England on a foreign tour. He failed to impress and blamed it on not having the right practice facilities. Yet others succeeded. It may be that a reliance on routine undermined his confidence. An over reliance on routine will always lead us to mental inflexibility. So rut hop!

I cannot understand why top coaches don't simply state that a development requirement of the contract that a player is offered is improved ability in these areas.

However, many young developing footballers, rugby players and cricketers could set their standards higher than the norm and know that that uniqueness would help them achieve their goals. Through developing ambidexterity they would make themselves more marketable. Why wait for coaches to demand it? (I don't believe for a minute that David Beckham waited for Sir Alec to suggest that he became a dead ball expert.) Why not simply make yourself the best you can be? You WILL reap the rewards!

So you've hopped out of a few ruts, you're growing your awareness everyday, how do you go about growing your self belief?

Cultivating powerful self belief

Will we ever know what is possible if we don't do it?

Will we ever do it if we don't think it's possible?

What if there is no limit to what is possible for us other than what we decide?

Sub 4 minute mile was impossible in everybody's mind until Roger Bannister and his team changed the mass consciousness. They just went for it.

What could you achieve if you believed it was possible? Is there really a limit to what you could achieve?

Have you ever tried building positive thoughts or self belief only to have your hopes dashed against the rocks of your own negativity? What did you do? Did you struggle on? Did you give up? Did you take a different tack? Did you win through in the end? Are you still using the power of your focused thoughts to achieve extraordinary things in your life or are you downgrading your expectations to avoid disappointment?

What is your philosophy on achievement? Is it a constructive and healthy one? Check. Write down what you think your view on achievement is. Then go for a walk or run.

Allow your mind to become absorbed in something else. Then come back and without looking at what you've previously written take a fresh, blank piece of paper and answer the question again. What is your philosophy on achievement?

Now compare your answers and see what you learn.

Please do not read on until you've done this exercise.

Many people will read this previous paragraph but not do the exercise. They will think that they've got the point. They have learnt the lesson intellectually but won't DO the exercise. These people are great dreamers but don't act upon their dream to achieve them. It is GREAT to dream, indeed we MUST allow ourselves to dream - if you can't dream it you can't achieve it! - but we must also have the courage to ACT if we wish to achieve our dreams and goals............................ .... so ....
...... DO IT ....
.... DO IT NOW .... go on........................
...... allow yourself to put this book down..............
.............then ....
.......write............................ run (or whatever)...........................
...........................write........... you'll be glad you did!

Did you do it before reading on?

If you did, well done, you are a dynamic person. Someone who already lives from courage. The simple yet powerful courage to take appropriate and effective action. You will have recognised that this may be an important and powerful exercise and that it is better to be effective than efficient - subtle but powerful distinctions.

Some people can be very busy all day, very efficiently completing tasks and taking actions that are simply not effective in getting them where they want to be.

You can be very efficient at being early for the number 9 bus when it's only the number 13 bus that will get you where you want to go.

Or as Steven Covey says *"you can be very efficiently climbing the ladder of success only to find that the ladder is leaning against the wrong wall!"* We will focus on targets and choosing direction in Chapter 5 but for now let's return to whether you did the exercise or not and, more importantly what that tells you about yourself.

If you wouldn't put this book down to do the exercise there may be a great realisation there for you about what your challenge in life is.

It may be that you're always rushing to the end. You may always be driven to know how it's going to turn out. This will tell you that you are result oriented, probably very impatient, probably quite tunnel-visioned, probably miss out on a lot of what's on offer every day as you rush from one situation to another always looking for more, never feeling fulfilled, always slightly dissatisfied, mostly too stressed to ever bother to stop and SEE and HEAR and FEEL what is **actually going on** rather than what you THINK you know is going on.

If you recognise some of that behaviour in you .... well done. In our society some of those characteristics are deemed not to be acceptable: impatience, rushing, missing out, stressed etc. so our normal defence mechanism is simply to blot them out. We leap straight into full scale denial. *"Not me I'm not impatient, no, not me .... anyway how much longer have we got to wait here?"*

If you don't recognise any of those characteristics in yourself, it may be that you have Mastered life. You will know because everything in your life is perfect, you will love everything about your life nothing ever is wrong. You are always deeply peaceful, happy, healthy, successful, abundant in everything good. You want for nothing physically, mentally, emotionally or spiritually.

On the other hand it may be that you're not very self aware yet. Perhaps you can see plenty of faults in others but not your own, yet. If you can't see your faults and weaknesses you can't fix or change them, so it would serve you well to go back to the top of page 11. Reread the bit on engaging your senses. Then spend a moment of quiet self reflection, choose one characteristic of your self that you would like to change or improve and silently imagine how you could do that. Then it's a simple choice as to whether you do or not. Your choice, as always. It's your life so it's your choice - whatever others may say! But if it's something that you wish to change or improve then why not just do it?

Openness is good, denial is destructive.

If you are in denial of anything it has control over you.

If you are in denial of anything it has control over you. So it is constructive and mature to be open to the possibility of say a negative or destructive behaviour pattern or mindset. Then you can look and see if there is something you want to change. Then change it. You can always ask how does this serve me? Or why would I want to be that way? When you realise that IT DOESN'T or I WOULDN'T then it is simply a decision to NOT DO THAT or NOT BE THAT WAY ANYMORE!!

Be who you want to BE. Not just in part but in every way. Be the best version of you that you can imagine. If you can imagine it, you can take small steps everyday to become that. BECOME that means come to BE that.

Simple. Ridiculously simple.

Letting go of doubt

If you try to cover over doubt with positive affirmations, or whatever, in order to build your confidence or self belief you are storing up trouble for later. Effectively you are burying it but not getting rid of it. Sweeping it under the carpet until the pile is so high you trip over it. And of course you're not blind! You know it's there. So as time goes on the effort of ignoring it or working around it becomes greater and more exhausting, until all your energy and strength goes into denying the existence of this doubt. Eventually the walls come crashing down. Your castle (self belief) built on sand crumbles.

There is a better way. Just let the doubt go. You can just let it go but many of you reading this will feel that may not be possible. It is BUT DON'T BELIEVE ME OR DISBELIEVE ME. TRY IT.

Then you will KNOW it works. Knowing is more powerful than believing.

England's cricket captain, Michael Atherton described being in, 'a state of both inertia and intense concentration, and I **knew** that I was in total control and they couldn't get me out.'

People used to say seeing is believing. It isn't. Seeing is seeing! And it's selective. We see what we want to see.

Don't believe it?

Boys, have you ever been shopping with a girl friend and afterwards (just to make you endure it for a second time) been asked what you thought of all those lovely dresses, or tops, or jackets, or suits, or jeans that you barely saw? Could you for the life of you remember what they looked like? No way! Yet, did you notice that girl? Oh the one in the faded jeans? What the one with blond hair right down her back? With the tight fitting, ribbed, red top, carrying some sort of jacket over her arm? Lovely figure, she was walking past us on the other side of the road, flicking hair back with her left hand and laughing at a joke from someone she was walking with?

No, didn't see her. I don't think so, couldn't be sure.

I hope I've made my point, (what was my point? Oh yes ...)

Scientists have estimated that seeing is 98% a brain function. The rods and cones (vision sensors) in our eyes are constantly presenting something like 2 billion pieces of information to the brain. It can't hack it. It really doesn't like that much work (would you?) So it chooses what it wishes to accept, it simplifies. For all the right reasons. Yet what you get to see uncannily tends to fit with your preconceived ideas about the world. If you have any! Most of us do. We don't like nasty little surprises so we try to figure everything out in advance - just to make sure. We then align everything to our preconceived ideas of what's what or we reject it .

Go into any English pub and sit quietly and listen. You will hear conversations where one person has a point of view and another person a different one. They can spend all night beating each other over the head with their opinion (which they have a right to) whilst never actually considering each other's opinion. They simply will not see what they don't already believe. Whether it's true or not!!!

When we are being brought up we will very often react to our parents wishes, guidelines, teachings, restrictions, limits whatever you choose to call them, by either falling in with them or rebelling against them. Thereby using 2 of the 360 degrees on the protractor of choice (actually there an infinite number). Sad.

Others enjoy parenting that encourages the young developing being to make their own choice with courage. Asking them what their heart tells them would be right for them regardless of what others may say or think, exploring healthy values and choices. These people are more likely to grow into adults who have the courage of their convictions, HAVE their own convictions indeed, and live purposeful lives, full of meaning and fulfilment and no need to infringe on or hurt others, open to new conditions, approaches, opinions etc. They become successful by their own measures.

So, getting back to letting go of doubt.
Well doubt seems a bit intangible, so how do you let go of something that is other than something physical. Let's see.

Ever been really angry with someone?

I mean REALLY angry.

Think of that time now. Bring back the memory. Can you get in touch with the feeling of being angry? Just allow the anger back into your body, where ever you feel your feelings. It might be your stomach or chest area.

Just allow that feeling of anger back in, which ever way it comes. It may be a gut wrenching anger, it may be mild irritation, a frustration, a niggle, a dissatisfaction, an annoyance, really pissed off, had enough, hacked off, can't believe it or just really mad, so cross, grrrrrh! Now ask yourself, who's this hurting? Them? Shouldn't think so, shouldn't think they know or care.

You? Yes, you bet. It's negative energy and it's dragging you down. It's on the back of your mind, your subconscious mind. It is HURTING YOU. Even if you are pretending it's not.

So what now? Do you want to hold on to it? Do you want to stuff hurt and anger back down and carry it around every where with you? Do you want this to continue hurting you in unseen ways (I guarantee it is)? Or would you prefer to simply decide to let it go? Just let it drift off into the ether.

Has it gone? Did you feel a slight energy shift? If the feeling seems to have gone, it has gone. It may be that you could do this letting go again to shift some other stuck energy. There may be more for you to let go of. Try it again now.

Here's a different way.

Sit comfortably in a seat and position where you can really relax.
Let go of any physical tension in your body and let go of anything you are holding on to. Let go of any thoughts as best you can and allow your awareness to settle on your breathing.
With your eyes either closed or open 'watch' the breath as it flows in and out through your nose. Feel yourself relaxing and becoming centred and focused on the breath that is entering and leaving your body. You don't need to do anything, it is all taking care of itself. It may help to imagine the breath as a coloured gas, whatever your favourite colour is, or a deep enriching purple gas or a revitalising orange one. But whatever works for YOU.

Now that you're relaxing, put your head down. Gently allow your head to drop onto your chest. Now imagine a great tap in the middle of your chest and open the tap to allow whichever negative emotion you would like to let go, to just easily and gently flow out of you.

Choose anything negative that you are holding onto and allow it to flow up out of your subconscious and away for good. If you're not sure whether you are holding onto something then just guess. Anger, sadness, fear, hurt, rejection, failure, arrogance are hidden deep so experiment. And enjoy. It feels fantastic to let go of any negativity. You feel lighter and better and more confident.

Do this letting go exercise for as long as you feel comfortable. It will serve you well to incorporate this as a regular part of your training and fitness routine. Being physically fit is only part of being prepared in this day and age. Mental and emotional strength are clearly factors that sports performers need and use in order to win, yet many talk about such requirements without the first idea of how they go about achieving mental or emotional fitness.

Anyone who has played under pressure will have sensed tension, in other players or the crowd. Not something you can really touch but real enough nevertheless.

So you now KNOW that you can release or let go negative emotions. Not because I said so, that would be believing hearsay - never an intelligent thing to do - but because you have experienced it

AND

YOU

KNOW.

While we're at it, a word on intelligence. Something that people misunderstand. Many people think intelligence is purely academic knowledge. It isn't, it's to do with capability within a given field. A carpenter, for example, may not seem to have intelligence if he has little general knowledge and does more drinking than point scoring in a pub quiz. Yet he has immense intelligence in his trade. Not just skill, but intelligence is required to understand the geometry, maths and other science needed in carpentry. Artistry too to work with raw materials, feel, aesthetic appreciation etc.

Many footballers have a great football brain - true intelligence in their field, this is true in all sports. Equally, I have come across football managers who are intelligent and those who are not. Some managers, great players in their time, have no intelligent way of relating to players in today's game. Motivating players a generation ago was different to how it is now. Intelligent managers know that and learn what they need to. Others, however, are one dimensional. If their preferred approach (often their only approach) doesn't work they have no answer other than get rid of the player. This often leaves them with a squad that is also one dimensional. A generation ago in English professional team sport it was effective to just bully players into performing. If they didn't do as you said, they could go back down the mine or back in the factory. Today, players have agents. You can't treat them like dirt and hope that will work. Well you can, but it won't. Times have changed. Player's expectations have changed. How you can treat people has changed. If you want to succeed you need a more intelligent approach.

So I have this definition:

Intelligent people are defined, not by what they think they know, but by what they are prepared to learn.

You see knowledge is an interesting phenomenon. People used to know that the world was flat. When you got to the edge you fell off. Now we know differently. Americans know that they won the second world war, just like they knew they were winning the Vietnam war and that all their boys were coming safely home. We English know that we built and developed Concorde (despite the obvious meaning of the name) and we know that we weren't duped into war with Iraq, we know our politicians wouldn't lie to us etc. etc. etc.

So if knowledge is not such a tangible product as we thought it was, then beliefs certainly are not.

So, we have established - or more importantly YOU have established (by experiencing it) that you can let go of intangible and non-physical things like feelings. Therefore you can now try for yourself the phenomenon of letting go of a belief. A belief is merely a thought that you have held for long enough to be convinced that it is true. **It may or may not be true but you think it is.**

So look at a belief such as doubting your ability. Try thinking of achieving something extraordinary. I'll give some suggestions. It doesn't matter whether you are professional or amateur, male or female, senior or junior.

Golfers: Will your self belief allow that you will score a hole in one every round you ever play from here on in? Not can, but WILL.

Cricketers: Will your self belief allow that you WILL score at least one double century every season? Bowlers that you will take at least one 10-fer in an innings every season?

Footballers: As a striker will your self belief allow that you will score a goal in every game for the next 12 months, again not could but WILL? Keepers, that you will keep a clean sheet for the next 12 months?

Rugby backs: that you will not mishandle for a year? Forwards that you'll never concede a turnover or infringe for a penalty for a year?

Those that I have missed I'm sure you get the idea. If these examples haven't done it come up with something that just splits your conscious mind and subconscious mind. You know like "I'd like to think I could but I'm not sure."

Now, recognise that little bit of self doubt and make the decision to let it go and see if there's any more to come up.

Use any of the techniques that I have described and think of this as you would of your physical training. The more you exercise this releasing 'muscle' the stronger and more responsive it will become.

If you need help or you think that you can't let go then e-mail our help desk at: pphelpdesk@martyncourt.co.uk

Alternatively buy the book 'The Sedona Method' by Hale Dwoskin available in good book shops or on-line from amazon. This book is excellent and the methods I use have been adapted from tools developed by Hale which he personally taught me, so he is the Master.

To close this chapter on self belief here are two more very useful tools to achieve the same desired state - massive levels of solid self belief working toward absolute self belief which is more a knowingness.

Whenever you get chance focus on your breathing and say (silently to your self) as you breathe out " I am breathing out doubt " and as you are breathing in " I am breathing in massive self belief ."

You can do this when exercising. Instead of occupying your mind with music or some other distraction use this technique. You may need to make it fit a faster breathing rhythm, so "doubt out,".........." deep belief in." Whatever fits or works for you.

You can do this anywhere any-time. If you are in a waiting room or driving or having dinner and are bored with the conversation (you might find that this increases your awareness and you will actually hear what's being said.) It's silent inside you and you don't need to close your eyes so no one will know that you are working your self belief muscle, except you. Oh, and your opponents next time you take the field of play a more focused, calm and self assured performer!

So breathe out doubt and breathe in self belief.

Do it now, treat yourself.

Before moving on to Chapter 4 take 5 minutes, or more, for you. Eyes closed or open, relax, focus on deep breathing. Breathe out doubt. Breathe in massive self belief. Indulge yourself for 5 minutes or more. It will change the depth of your self belief. It will improve your future performances.

BREATHE OUT DOUBT.

BREATHE IN MASSIVE SELF BELIEF.

Again,

BREATHE OUT ALL SELF DOUBT.

BREATHE IN LIMITLESS SELF BELIEF.

Again,

BREATHE OUT ALL SELF DOUBT.

BREATHE IN LIMITLESS SELF BELIEF.

Again,

BREATHE OUT ALL SELF DOUBT.

BREATHE IN LIMITLESS SELF BELIEF.

Again,

BREATHE OUT ALL SELF DOUBT.

BREATHE IN LIMITLESS SELF BELIEF.

Again,

BREATHE OUT ALL SELF DOUBT.

BREATHE IN LIMITLESS SELF BELIEF.

Again,

BREATHE OUT ALL SELF DOUBT.

Now,

BREATHE IN LIMITLESS SELF BELIEF.

4 Other levels of consciousness

"Sooner or later in sport we run into situations that are too big for us to master...... as a result sport leads to the most remarkable self discovery." - **Roger Bannister**

There are many levels of consciousness. For many people they are very aware of their conscious mind, aware that they have a subconscious mind but their curiosity stops there.

The conscious mind

The conscious or rational mind is what sceptics identify with. It is our ego mind. It is what we use to analyse situations with. Very useful if used correctly. However, many people don't use their mind - their mind uses them!! Have you ever come across people who are obsessive thinkers? You can't say anything without them having to question everything. They cannot accept anything, they have to pull it apart, argue with it (or you) for no particular purpose. Now I'm not saying this ability isn't useful. It is. But these people are operating from a program that runs them, not using the rational mind to move them forward to what they desire. This is often referred to as 'Analysis Paralysis'. The key is that the mind must work FOR you not AGAINST you. You must be its Master not its slave (well you don't have to but it is mad not to!)

Sceptics are people who over-identify with the rational mind. They don't take anything on faith. If it can't be explained they won't believe it's possible. Yet the prison they create for themselves is disappointment and lack of fulfilment. You see, the conscious mind works from past experience. Therefore being over-identified with the conscious mind would mean that you are unable to believe, with sufficient commitment to make it true, vastly new concepts. You would dismiss them as 'impossible'.

People who have changed the status quo, who have taken mankind forward in extraordinary steps used their subconscious mind to get there. And indeed anyone who has performed miracles in the field of sporting endeavour or simply been 'pretty bloody good' has (whether they know it or not) used the conscious mind to set themselves fulfilling targets then emptied the subconscious mind of negative, self defeating thoughts and belief patterns and basically trusted their conscious practice to have grooved the subconscious in what is required then let it loose and stood back and admired the results.

The subconscious mind

Our creativity comes from our higher levels of consciousness. The key with the subconscious mind is to get it on your side. Get it working with you to achieve the conscious targets and desires that you have set.

How do you do that?

Well in order to get someone willingly on your side you need to know their agenda. What is the subconscious mind's agenda and indeed what is it? The subconscious or unconscious mind is simply all the thoughts that we are not looking at in the moment. Useful things and not so useful things.

Useful thoughts, behaviour patterns, preferences, memories and held onto emotions are easy to spot. The necessary yet mundane bodily functions like breathing, beating the heart, blinking our eyes etc. are largely put onto auto pilot in the subconscious. This is constructive. Good, supporting, happy memories and experiences are stored there too. That's fine. The problems arise when we have stored destructive or undermining memories or belief patterns there. It is a problem because we are not looking at them. If we saw them we would say, *"Woa that's not helping or serv-*

ing me I'm going to get rid of that." However, because they are hidden from our view we can't throw them out and they continue to affect our performance for the worse.

So that's what the subconscious mind is; just thoughts, emotions, beliefs and habituated behaviour patterns. It doesn't exist in physicality. The brain is an organ that the mind uses but it is not the mind. If a brain was transplanted into a new body it would not contain any of the thoughts and memories of the previous owner. The new owner would not suddenly have tastes for things that he/she had previously found repulsive nor would they have memories of a childhood that was not their own. The mind is not physically there.

When a body dies, you can do as many autopsies as you wish you will never find the mind or indeed the spirit of the being that occupied that body.

So, that's what the mind is. What is its agenda? Well it's intention is to help you. It wants the best for you, it wants to help you survive. It's just that it's got some bloody funny ideas about that.

Not its fault. The ideas have been put in there every moment of every day since you were knee high to a grasshopper. Not its fault. I was told, all my young life 'those who ask don't get'. My subconscious heard it often enough that it believed it. Bless its little cotton socks!

Why was I told that? Who knows. Who cares! I now know that those who don't ask DON'T get. Those who ASK get.

So now if I want something I ask, sometimes I get, sometimes I don't. That's all there is to know.

So it is a good idea to check out what is lurking in there to see what serves us. What doesn't, we can let go of. After all if we let go of what drags us down we will be lighter and more effective. A good thing to be.

THE FOUNDATION FOR EFFECTIVE ACTION IS TO HAVE INTEGRITY. By that I mean to have both the conscious and subconscious mind aligned. When you have aligned thought then you step into the fray with real power. You have decided on your desired outcome - consciously, and there is nothing in your subconscious that weakens that resolve. There are no conflicting thoughts or beliefs. Like a laser beam, your intention is concentrated, focused and directed. And like a laser beam it will cut through the toughest opposition.

Whenever you so align these two levels of consciousness you are close to becoming in the 'zone'. And whenever you are aligned you invoke, or tap into, the superconscious.

The superconscious mind

This phenomenon is one that most sports performers have experienced by accident. Perhaps you have experienced it but until now didn't have a label for it. Of course there are many who haven't. Certainly I have heard players talking about 'the zone' with clearly no knowledge of what they are talking about.

Yet this state or phenomenon exists. Those who have experienced it KNOW it exists. Formerly an England Test cricketer and captain, currently TV commentator David Lloyd told me of his experience of the 'Zone'. He was at Cheltenham walking toward the pavilion musing that someone must have had a good day as the scoreboard clearly showed that a batsman had 195 runs to his name. It began to dawn on him that THAT batsman was himself! He had just lost his wicket but regained his conscious awareness. It was him, HE had made 195 against a very strong Gloucestershire side but had been in such a 'zone' of focused concentration that he could not be aware of it until he came out of it.

Sceptics doubt the phenomenon because they haven't yet experienced it and as you know they doubt anything that cannot be seen, smelled, heard, tasted or touched. They believe what they believe and that's fair enough but YOU are not like that. You are opening your mind more and more. And YOU will be able to experience this more powerful state because you are opening to it.

I KNOW THIS because you wouldn't be reading this if you weren't open to new concepts. If you were stuck in arrogance, complacency or apathy you would be 'satisfied' with being good enough already. But you're not. You deeply desire to constantly and consistently explore ways of becoming the best you can be. You are open to the possibility that there are no limits on your ability other than those you place upon yourself. You are, therefore, open to any technique that could help you become the best version of you.

Now I know it may seem to you that that's not the way you have always been. So what! It is the way you are becoming. In any - no EVERY - moment it is WHAT YOU ARE in that moment that counts, not WHAT YOU HAVE BEEN or indeed WHAT YOU THINK YOU WILL BE.

Being fully in the NOW MOMENT is a powerful state in itself and invokes the power of the superconscious.

What do you need to do to be fully in the now?

Well, ... take your mind off the past or future.

When you try to do that you will see that your mind is almost constantly in the past or the future.

How do you do that? How do you get right into the NOW?

Remember the exercise for growing your awareness? Do that. Fully engage your senses, really feel the moment, notice every thing about it. Your mind can only do a few things, consciously, at the same time so by bringing its attention to your senses (or bringing it to its senses) it shuts up. It can't do all that negative stuff like; judging things, complaining, being dissatisfied, worrying about the future, regretting the past etc. etc.

We sometimes do this spontaneously when we are struck with awe by the beauty of some natural phenomenon like a beautiful sunset. The reason it seems so gorgeous is that at last your mind has SHUTUP! You have no thoughts running mad around your mind, you are just witnessing this awesome spectacle. You are speechless and thoughtless. You are simply a witness to something of unspeakable beauty. You are calm and deeply peaceful. In that moment you want for nothing. All problems seem insignificant in that moment, so much so that they cease to exist for you. Everything IS perfect.

I am a left handed opening bat. My batting seems to have that effect on people. It leaves them speechless and mind numbed. It is unspeakable!!

So these are ways that you can tap into the superconscious which is 'the zone' that many have experienced and many more talk about but have not experienced.

BUT WHAT IS IT?

A way I like to describe it is:
It is like an internet of the mind, a sort of linking of all minds, or even all souls or beings.

Some may find it hard to imagine but most people have had experiences that they cannot explain and often put down to extraordinary coincidence or just dismiss as 'spooky'. That's fine. But WHAT IF it does exist as a phenomenon? Those who have experienced it KNOW it exists. Some actively and consciously use it.

In his book The Inner Game of Tennis, Tim Gallwey refers to this phenomenon as Self 3. He has used this tool to help top tennis players to reach heights of performance they would not have conceived of as possible.

As I previously mentioned you can tap into this resource by quieting the noise in the mind, i.e. all the conflicting and warring thoughts. You will have seen people striving to gain or be something and it seems an effort. This is a clear sign that an inner struggle is occurring, whereas you will also see people easily achieving their desires. You could think they are lucky - and they are. Yet to dismiss luck as uncontrollable is to miss the point. If you believe that though, IT WILL BE TRUE FOR YOU! As you think so shall you be.

You will notice that lucky people think they ARE lucky, wealthy people know they ARE wealthy, unlucky people know they ARE unlucky (they keep telling you don't they?), depressed people know they ARE depressed (they keep on and on and on telling you) and, of course, winners know they ARE winners, even if they lose a battle they KNOW they will win the war. The defining feature here is that these people don't WANT. They don't WANT what they have - THEY JUST HAVE IT!

What's the point?

The point is you have to hold the attitude **that you are having** what you choose to have or **you are becoming** what you wish to be. So having learned to let go of emotions and beliefs and thoughts that don't serve you, here is a new challenge: TO LET GO OF WANTING and allow yourself to HAVE. You see wanting means lacking. You don't want something you have - YOU HAVE IT.

To make it even more powerful instead of holding the **thought** that you are becoming what you wish to be (successful, the best in your team/ league/country/world/history of mankind/whatever) you can now experiment with holding the **feeling of already being** what or how you wish to be.

Try it now, remember a success that you have had - the biggest one you can think of - and now remember what it felt like. Remember how it felt in your body, how it put a spring in your step, a sparkle in your life, remember how warm and contented you felt. Really allow yourself to feel that way again, now. Now allow yourself to hold that feeling and see how long you can hold it for. Write the time down, then challenge yourself over the next week to see what your world record in any day is for holding the feeling of being massively successful. DO IT. It is a critical and powerful skill. And it is a learnable skill.

In all sports the top level of players can all play. What sets the winner apart from the rest is their acquired ability to use, for extended periods, these emotional, mental and spiritual skills. FACT!

SO, LETTING GO OF WANTING IS A CRITICAL SKILL IN ENABLING PERFORMERS TO HOLD IN MIND THAT WHICH THEY DESIRE TO HAVE OR BECOME.

Practice now with one of the methods you have learned. Here's a cue:

Ask yourself this question and answer it honestly.

Can I allow myself to let go of any sense of wanting success (or your goal) and simply allow it to come to me?

and/or

Would I rather WANT success or HAVE it? (you will understand now that you can't have something AND want it)

Continue to experiment with this. EVERY TIME YOU ASK YOURSELF SUCH A QUESTION YOU ARE REPROGRAMMING YOUR SUBCONSCIOUS MIND AND ACTIVATING THE SUPERCONSCIOUS.

If you are not constantly letting go of negativity it is as though you are pumping hot air into the balloon of your ambition but also adding more bags of ballast with each blast of the burner. There will be a lot of energy expended, a lot of strain on everything but you won't fly. So by all means use positive affirmations but drop the ballast too!!

Letting go of wanting is getting into some very subtle refining or reprogramming of the subconscious mind. It is eradicating negativity. Yet if you want to be the best you can be this will take you beyond what others are capable of.

A way in which it could benefit you is; those who are desperate to win can fall foul of 'trying too hard'. Wanting to win wouldn't exist if you KNEW you were going to win. So, subtly, wanting to win is coming from a fear that you won't win and as such is very deep, yet very subtle, self doubt. You see this in teams or players who freeze on the big occasions. So knowing that, why would you ever WANT to win? You would just take the field of play with the calm, centred and focused attitude that you KNOW that you COULD win, you KNOW that you ARE good enough, you KNOW that if you produce your best you WILL win.
So your challenge is to remain relaxed yet focused and DELIVER your optimum performance level. If that is good

enough you'll win. If it isn't, you will have increased your awareness of where you need to improve your performance level so that you can continue enjoying the process of becoming as good as you can be. And maybe - just maybe - there are **no limits** to how good you can be. You will have healthy attitudes toward your opponent/s. They help you to set your standards until you are so far ahead of everyone else that you have to do that for yourself. So you would be grateful for good opposition, they make becoming the best you can be more fun. They are merely a challenge not an obstacle.

Winston Churchill said, *"Pessimists see obstacles, optimists see opportunities."*

So, letting go of wanting will make it easier to hold the feeling you desire AS THOUGH IT HAS ALREADY BEEN ACHIEVED. This will help you open to the superconscious. Being open to the superconscious will mean you will benefit in ways that the conscious mind would not believe possible. The conscious mind tries to project into the future based on its experiences of the past. It wants to keep you in a comfort zone to help you feel secure. 'Stick with what you know' kind of ethic. Of course if you wish to expand your possibilities this doesn't help.

Footballers I have worked with talk of being in the flow or zone and 'reading' the intention of an opponent. This is telepathy. It comes through being open to the superconscious. It is not guesswork and it is not luck and the player didn't try to do it. The more you are open to it the more frequently you will experience it.

When players have experienced this phenomenon it is only after the event that they realise that THEY KNEW exactly what was going to happen. It wasn't a conscious thought or a verbal message in the mind. It was simply a KNOWING.

Cricketers know that you cannot have the conscious conversation with yourself that would be required to assess the pace, line, length, bounce (rate of climb or otherwise), swing or other deviation of a delivery and then the choice of where the gaps in the field are so as to choose where to direct the shot, in the 0.4 of a second that you have to respond to an 80 m.p.h. delivery. What happens is you consciously practice shots until they are programmed into your subconscious mind and IT brings them out at the appropriate moment. The best thing you can do is get your conscious (fear based or ego) mind out of the way and trust and allow your subconscious mind to trot out what you practised. From here what dictates the nature of the innings is the amount of courage the batsman has to play the more attacking shots from his/her subconscious locker. This is often drawn externally from captains instructions or a perception of the state of the game at that moment. However, we are each in charge of our own perceptions. So both batsmen in any given partnership are experiencing fairly similar conditions and circumstances yet both may be employing different levels of aggression dependant on their perception. This is in turn dependant on that player's courage/confidence.

Where this is demonstrated significantly is in the way that the Australian batsmen have had the courage to 'up the ante' and set a new standard of run rate in Test match cricket. This has changed the modern game as much as Clive Lloyd's tactic a generation ago of using four pace bowlers to dominate world cricket, did then. This has less to do with technique and much more to do with mental skills.

A good friend of mine is Steve Adshead of Gloucestershire County Cricket Club. He is becoming one of the best wicketkeeper/batsmen that English cricket has seen. He talks about being in the flow or zone when batting and it seeming like time stops. He says he experiences moments where the ball just sits up and waits for him to 'slap' it to the boundary. It is being open to the superconscious that pro-vides these very real experiences. I was sat with friends at a football game recently when a striker scored from about 35 yards.

That in itself wasn't so remarkable as much as everybody in the crowd around us KNEW it was going to happen. It was as though someone slowed the film reel down except that this was live action. It may be that everybody at that game (Cheltenham Town v York City 1-1) had the same momen-tary 'slow motion PREplay' certainly everyone within dis-cussion distance of us experienced it. Yes we were seeing the future. We were receiving advance knowledge through the superconscious. Most people would probably dismiss it. Yet if you are open to the possibility, these experiences will become more frequently a part of your experience.

When Nathan Astle scored his remarkable double century against England he was dancing down the wicket to Andy Caddick and hitting him back over his head, out of the ground for 6. You can't do that! .... not to Andy Caddick, his pace, the steepness of bounce because of his height, YOU CAN'T DO IT!!..............
...........UNLESS................. you are in the zone (he said he was) and therefore the superconscious is feeding you a **knowingness** about where the bowler is going to bowl it.

Now, I don't believe Nathan Astle knows why or how he was able to achieve that because he hasn't managed to, con-sistently, since. (I don't know, I'm guessing because he declined my interview). However, he could easily do it again and again if he learned the tools of putting himself in that state. If he did it once it must be possible to do it again. More importantly if he could do it, then anyone else could do it.

So keep experimenting and being open to the possibility of this resource. It is real. It is powerful and it will become your ally in achieving world class results. Let's now look at a powerful and fresh approach to targeting or goal setting.

5 A new model for goal setting

*" The unconscious feeling of reaching a goal almost always wins over the conscious will." * - **Willi Railo**

There have been many models for goal setting, some more effective than others. I am sure you must have your own, though it may be ad hoc or accidental and not as effective as it could be. Worse, you may have a method that actually works against what you are trying to achieve. A prime example is how SMART goals can undermine what you are trying to achieve.

Many well meaning 'motivation gurus' or 'time management/achievement consultants' have taught this model. In case you don't know it, it stands for something like:

S	-	specific
M	-	measurable
A	-	achievable
R	-	realistic
T	-	time specific

Now, there are good reasons why this works and many people have succeeded using this model, however, it has some implied pitfalls. Smart Goals were developed as a business tool to control employee performance. Their main purpose is to control. When motivating yourself to higher performance control can bring up resistance and make your goal seem a chore or duty rather than a joy. I prefer my model (obviously) for reasons that will become apparent. The SMART model can have this effect:

S	-	for specific	read	- LIMITING
M	-	for measurable	read	- LIMITING
A	-	for achievable	read	- LIMITING
R	-	for realistic	read	- LIMITING
T	-	for time specific	read	- LIMITING

The model I propose is similar yet immensely more powerful, due to subtle differences.

Progress/process goals and result goals

One of the tricks many people miss is that of setting progress goals. This is not the same as action steps towards goals. These are powerful targets in their own right and avoid the pain caused by result goals which can lead to frequent failure and destruction of confidence.

Progress goals (or process - same thing) are goals that can be achieved in every practice or contest situation in fact ANY situation. They don't necessarily have a time frame and you can make them 'unfailable'.

An example would be: "I am improving my strength, fitness and flexibility in every way, every day."

This is not impossible to fail but even rest-days could be moving you towards this goal. Many people have this sort of goal implied but not expressed. It is powerful though, to acknowledge these unwritten goals, review and write them down. A diary or journal is useful. I use a pocket sized note pad labelled 'goals and gains' to record goals achieved (this builds self worth, confidence and self belief) and to write new goals in. This is a powerful tool. I recommend you use one but keep it private.

Another progress goal could be: " With every breath I grow my self confidence and self belief."

And: " *I now treat all practice as though it were a match situation.*"
So why do I not like the SMART model?

SPECIFIC

I don't like to be too specific because it can limit upward potential. In cricket many batsmen get out on exactly 50 or exactly 100 why? It's mad. There are similar parallels in all sports. Target achieved, focus and concentration waiver whilst the mind is looking for a new guideline. The mind is rudderless. Determination to achieve the goal is satisfied, focus now is not sure what to focus on. While you are in this mental no man's land the opposition have scored a goal or the bowler has nipped one back and you're staring at the pavilion wondering why or how you're heading back there! So I prefer an open ended no limit goal like: *"I allow myself to score AT LEAST 50 runs today."*

Once you are scoring 50s fairly regularly you can up the target but keep it to a target that you can believe so AT LEAST 60 might be right for you. **Only you can know what's right for you.** You may start higher or lower but start where it is appropriate. You may start with your last performance and build from there.

If you are a footballer, you may be a wide playing midfielder. You could look at your last game. HONESTY is required (after all you can lie to everybody, if you wish, but lying to your self is just plain stupid - extreme self deceit, denial or delusion is described as clinical mental illness - but it's just mad, it's stupid, why on earth would you want to do that? STOP IT NOW!)

So, you've honestly assessed your last performance and you realise that over the entire 90 minutes you've only delivered ONE quality ball into the danger area. There were a couple of crosses that went out of play and some didn't beat the first man. You put all temptation to blame the conditions, your team mates, the boss, the opposition, the game plan, your parents or whatever, aside for now. No blame for you. You're becoming a mature professional!! So you notice that you did a great deal of tackling back and defending but you need to up your creative and attacking output.

At the next team meeting you suggest, without hint of blame, that if we could defend 10 yards further up the park then you will do your best to increase the quantity of quality balls into the danger area. You work all week just going the extra mile in terms of skill practice. You may resolve to teach yourself to deliver equally well with both feet within 2 months. You may set the target that all your crosses will stay in play. You will deliver AT LEAST TWO quality balls in EACH half as well as all the tackling back etc. Then after your next game you will assess your performance against those goals and go through the process again. Very few pro players are that committed to their club or ultimately to their own career. The world is full of players (of all sports) who did just enough until it was too late, then spend their retirement telling the ever dwindling group of people who will listen, how good they could have been IF this or IF that.

Is that how you would like to be or are you absolutely committed to being the best you could be?

Oh dear, I feel like I've just gone off on one there!!

Back to SMART goals.

MEASURABLE

This is really introducing the ability of objective appraisal. Essential when you are a manager or employer paying bonuses against target related performance etc. However, when you are aiming to build your own self belief you need to develop objective feedback and honest but constructive appraisal too. Catching yourself doing something right is powerful so long as you don't ignore areas you can improve. Process goals have success built in, this is what winners do. They catch themselves winning. It's been said that Ian Botham was never out. It was never his fault, there was always a reason why he got out. Sight screen, dazzled by a car windscreen or all sorts. Now I'm not criticising. I admire the great man's achievements, fighting spirit and sheer entertainment value and unshakeable will to win, we could do with a dozen with those strengths now. Yet I wouldn't recommend it as a method for anyone other than him because one day you just might question the truth of it. You might think that your confidence is built on lying to yourself and I think that might feel awfully uncomfortable.

So I recommend honest feedback.

ACHIEVABLE

The danger to avoid is that 'achievable' can be misinterpreted as realistic which can be interpreted as limited in some way. I understand that if the target seems too far away it can be a de-motivator. Not constructive. What I like to see is it stretching you as much as you can in a constructive and positive way.

REALISTIC

You know my thoughts on this. Anything deemed realistic to the sceptic is often merely an excuse to be negative. Have you noticed how pessimists always justify their negativity by labelling it 'realism'? Yet of course this is down to individual perception or choice. Ask yourself the question could it get any worse? And the answer is of course YES. Now ask yourself the question could it get any better? Again the answer is YES. So it's not the answer that's important. IT'S THE QUESTION THAT'S IMPORTANT.

There are people running around looking for answers. What a waste of time. If you were **meant** to know the answer you **would**.

What's more powerful is asking the right questions. This is a classic rule of success. The person asking the question is usually the one with the power. So get into the habit of asking YOURSELF the RIGHT QUESTIONS.

Questions like:
Can I be better today than I was yesterday?
Can I allow myself more self belief today than ever before?
Can I allow myself to be more relaxed, more focused, more effective, more aware with every moment?

Stuff like that.

Finally,

TIME FRAMED

Again, this can be limiting. Be careful. Your goal may be to stay focused for the full 90 minutes of a game of football. Change it to 'until the game is over'. Losing to a goal in the 93rd minute is galling in the extreme!

My New model

So what elements make for a powerful goal setting model?

Unlimitedness, powerful positive motivation (fear doesn't work beyond a certain limit), a clear idea of the desired outcome, being set in the present as opposed to future or past and a capacity for honest constructive feedback as a link to progressive and expandable goals.

So here I shall suggest a new model.

HAPPI GOALS!

Now, you may think that this sounds a bit soppy but there is a very powerful and profound psychological reason for this particular mnemonic.

If you look back to see why you became any good at the sport that you are looking to gain an advantage in you will see that there was something about it that you loved and that THAT made you happy.

I have worked with so many professional team sport players who have performed perfectly well until the last year of their contract. Then they take their eye off the ball - so to speak - they put pressure on themselves to perform, in so doing they stop enjoying the game and it becomes like a chore. This rapidly becomes a downward spiral of trying harder and achieving less.

It may be that you loved a particular technique or skill. It may be you loved the team or individual element. It may be you loved the physical or mental challenge. Maybe the competition, the winning. Or it may be that you loved the game or entertaining others through it.

Whatever!

The point is: that the POINT IS - you need to LOVE it in order to be your best and THAT will make you happy.

So .... HAPPI GOALS!

HAPPI goals will have these elements:

Honesty - in appraising your own performance
and in positive feedback
Absolute certainty of outcome
Present tense
Passion
Infinite possibility

So, this is how you make it work for you.

Say you are a cricketer, a batsman and last year you averaged 32, you made three 50s and one 100. You may wish to improve all of those stats. So here are goals that will make you HAPPI:

I am becoming a higher scoring batsman

I love averaging at least 33, making at least four 50s and converting at least one of those into at least a 100.

Then having established your overall goal for the season you can set some process goals (you probably noticed that 'I am becoming a higher scoring batsman' is in fact a process goal) for example:

I love treating all practice as if it were match situation.

I really love all fitness training and skill practice.

I love being relaxed, in a thought free zone and loving scoring runs.

I love improving in all areas of my life.

I love growing my confidence to play more aggressively/attacking shots.

I love being physically relaxed yet having absolute mental focus.

You will notice that not all of these goals have all the elements of HAPPI in them, it's not mandatory yet the ethic of why you try to include these elements is this.

HONESTY

By honesty here I mean, objective feedback. There is no room for immaturity in either false modesty, self deprecating, defeatist or any other negative judgement. Or indeed false optimism or ego pumping. Words like rubbish, useless etc. or brilliant, fantastic etc. are emotional judgements not objective awareness. As a bowler, if you slope one down the leg side and your self-talk is 'that's rubbish', you are likely to make yourself try harder which will bring you out of the 'state of optimum performance'. Worse you will probably be holding in mind, 'I don't want to **bowl another down leg**' and guess what - you probably will because you're focusing on **bowling down leg**. How often do you see that? Yet it's not bloody rocket science! YOU GET WHAT YOU FOCUS ON!

So, acknowledge that the ball was not bad, merely not where you intended. Assess it objectively; the length may have been what you intended, there may have been good pace, so the only adjustment required is the line. Similarly, you may bowl a delivery that is hit for runs.

You remain focused and acknowledge that the delivery was 3 inches wider than you intended, everything else was okay so you focus on the area that you intend to bowl - 3 inches nearer off stick - and, staying physically relaxed yet absolutely focused you run in again and hit the spot. This time you're in the area of uncertainty and the batsman has to take a risk to play it. Again you assess the delivery, no histrionics about how great you are or how lucky the batter was. Just an assessment and switch back to focus for the next ball. You can switch off (a little) when you're not bowling but for now **just do what you do and STAY IN THE MOMENT**.

ABSOLUTE CERTAINTY OF OUTCOME

This ensures that you stay focused. It goes without saying that if you're not sure of what you want out of a situation it's unlikely that you'll get it. However, that's quite superficial. When I say ABSOLUTE I mean a vision of outcome that has no hold-back in ANY way, on any of the levels on which we live.

People often hold dreams, that on a subconscious - sometimes even conscious level - they don't believe is possible or that they deserve. This hold-back is usually sufficient to keep them disappointed for years before giving up with some 'philosophical' lie like, *"oh I never really wanted it."* Sad.

So it's vital here to test out your goal to see if there is any subconscious resistance to it. Write your goal and look at it. Let's use an example:

I love becoming the best (whatever your sport is) man/woman in the world.

This should stir up some resistance if there is any! If you are David Beckham, Jonny Wilkinson, Glenn McGrath or Clive Woodward you may wish to try this:

I love exploring just how good I could be and continuing to be the best in the world.

Anyhow, write your personal goal out. Read it to yourself, out loud if possible, and see what comes up. There maybe some doubt.

Ask yourself if this doubt helps you and make the decision to let it go. (It doesn't help you, holding on to doubt weakens your power to achieve.) Ask yourself if there's any reason why you don't think you could or should achieve this goal. Whatever that hold back, resistance or negative thought or feeling - Let it go. Use one of the techniques that you learnt and practised before.

IF YOU HAVEN'T USED ANY OF THOSE TECHNIQUES EXPLAINED EARLIER I WOULD SUGGEST YOU LOOK AT YOUR COMMITMENT TO YOURSELF. It would appear that you don't take yourself seriously. Or perhaps you feel you can have the improvement without actually making any changes. Treat yourself, learn these letting go techniques. You'll never know if you don't try.

Be patient but be thorough. Keep reading out the goal and letting go of anything that comes up until it feels as though it's just a formality. There should be no pull from the goal. You may start off believing you can have the goal (or not) but when you've fully released on the goal it should feel like it's already happened. There are just no further issues around it. You're going to love doing your best but either it will happen or it won't. If you've ever negotiated from that position you will know how powerful, almost irresistible that state is.

If after completing the book and practising these techniques for a while you feel you need some support please e-mail: ppsupport@martyncourt.co.uk

PRESENT TENSE

This is simple, there are two very good reasons why you should ALWAYS set your goals in the present tense.

Firstly, many people set goals in the future 'I would love to be......' The problem here is it is too easy to keep them in the future and never achieve them. The only time we ever achieve anything is NOW.

Secondly, if you say *"I love being the best I can be"* and on some subtle level you don't think you are, or you can be, or you don't deserve to be or any of the millions of negative thoughts or feelings we can be hiding in our subconscious then this encourages them to come to the surface so we can decide to let them go.

PASSION

As a motivator there is nothing more powerful than loving to do something. Don't believe me, just look back over your life. Have you ever turned down various opportunities because you were too busy? Only to have the opportunity to do something you love turn up and ....
........suddenly you're not too busy any more. If we think we should get fit, lose a bit of weight, do our homework etc. we will struggle to find the time and energy, it saps us. We may get it done at the last minute but it never flows. If on the other hand we love what we do, nothing ever gets in the way. We do it in a constructive way. It makes us happy so we give the best version of ourselves to those that are around us. It's a win win situation. Of course, sometimes the people close to us don't have our best interests at heart. That may be something we have to deal with. It may be their envy of our success makes them want to sabotage our goals but usually they too would love us to do well. I went to do some work with a very talented pro snooker player who couldn't get past the last 16. On referring to his advisors he decided not to go ahead. Could they possibly have had his best interests at heart? Possibly, but whatever, he still hasn't got past the stage he gets stuck at. Shame, he may need to change his so called support group if he would LOVE to win a major tournament.

Many people use fear as their motivation, fear of failing, fear of looking stupid, going broke, whatever. It works, up to a point. Somehow I feel it is a shame though because it has underlying negative connotations. People who use fear often become very dark when things go wrong. They become bad losers get spiteful, surly, cheat.

I just don't believe, from my experiences, that it is the best way. If you haven't tried it try it now. Put love into your goals and what you're trying to achieve in all areas of your life.

Try it, you might like it.

INFINITE POSSIBILITY

Okay, it's a big concept for some people but what I'm suggesting is: what if there is no limit other than the limit you put on yourself?

Well of course this may or may not be true but what if it was TRUE? Then wouldn't you want some? What if you could achieve something that no human had ever done before? Wouldn't that be good beyond your own personal achievement and satisfaction? Wouldn't that act as a beacon of inspiration to all others on the planet? Let's face it if everyone was busy loving their everyday, enjoying exploring how good they could be at something they love, there wouldn't be a lot of time left for being nasty to anyone (of course their self esteem and self respect would be so high they wouldn't want to anyway). You may think that's idealist but actually it is the logical result of inspiring people to be the best they can be.

So, in these goals you will notice that I say 'AT LEAST' at least every time I set a goal!! It's simple but it works TRY IT. You are opening to the possibility that you don't even know what you're capable of BUT YOU'RE OPEN TO, AND HAVE THE COURAGE TO, EXPLORE IT.

So experiment, have fun and allow your goals to be HAPPI ones and just see how happy they make you. Stick with it, write them down, keep them private unless you know who you share them with will support not undermine you, monitor your progress and tweak your goals. As soon as you have achieved one, acknowledge your success in some way, tick it off and write a new one.

If you would like feedback on goals you've set, send your written goals and a cheque for £60 made out to: Martyn Court - goal support.

To: Martyn Court - Goal Support
        Trafford Publishing (UK) Limited
        Enterprise House
        Wistaston Road Business Centre
        Crewe
        CW2 7RP
        UK

You will receive comments on your goals and suggestions on how to make them more powerful if you are new to this style of goal setting.

Well, having set your goals you now need to put them to work.

Just like that new lawn-mower won't cut the grass if it's left in the shed, so too these tools need to be used.

The way you will most usefully use them is to simply hold them in mind. Writing them down is essential but it's only a start. To have these desires actually turn up in your life, to have these changes actually occur you need to take action. Not any old action but right action aligned to your goal. So you need to hold them in mind.

To do that effectively we use single pointed attention or focus. That is the next chapter

6 Single pointed focus

"Make every obstacle an opportunity." - **Lance Armstrong**

Somewhere in the Bible it says *"As you think so shall you be"*. The same message is given in many other sayings, wisdoms, texts etc.

IT IS TRUE.

Yet again I say, **don't believe me**, try it. Try it now. Think of the most peaceful place you've ever been to..really see it in your mind's eye ....remember what it smells like .... hear the sounds ....hear everything... not just the most obvious, immediate sounds ....hear the things nearby ....and hear the sounds in the background .... now listen to the silent gaps between the sounds ....enjoy the view all over again ....feel the richness of the colours ....let them wash over you .... feel the peace settling around you like a warm comfort blanket ....feel the peace at least as much as you did back then ....drop into that feeling of peace ....feel like you're floating .... being supported by the sheer strength of this deep ....

.... endless...........
................................PEACE.

69

If you found yourself drawing almost involuntary deep breaths. If you found yourself gently smiling to yourself, almost despite yourself. If you found yourself relaxing and dropping into a deeper sense of peace. Then you have just proved to yourself some key truths:

As you think so shall you be.

You co-create your own reality, starting with the power of your thoughts.
You DO have control over how you feel (you no longer need react to anyone else's emotional manipulating). Of course it's true that you could choose to make yourself feel the worst you've ever felt too; depressed, unloved, useless, ill, whatever! BUT WHY THE HELL WOULD YOU WANT TO DO THAT?

Yes I know people do. Yes they do. But that's only because they can still find people who get off on feeling superior by dishing out sympathy to people. These people usually despise the weakness (or weak one) they're sympathising with. Sympathy can be a drug that people dish out. Like crack cocaine it's profitable to deal in. The profit is feeling better at someone else's expense. They become addicted so keep coming back for more. So it's a soft market - no hard sell required. Addicts love their pushers and dealers. Can't wait for their next fix. Sadly, the cure for a sympathy addict is rare. It's called compassion. Most people don't have it or even understand what it is. Even if they did most don't have the courage to administer it. You see with compassion you would want to help, not fuel the addiction but offer help to cure it. You would take courageous action like gently helping them to see their addiction and supporting them in their action to help themselves. This is dangerous work. Depressives, don't always react pleasantly when their self obsession is pointed out. Smokers, drug addicts, anorexics and bulimics don't react to you well when you highlight that they must hate themselves to be so actively

70

killing themselves! Fat people think you're 'being nasty' when you point out the stark staring bloody obvious that they eat more than their body needs or very often that their life is so dull that they've become obsessed with eating. (This great paradox is sad but funny - people trying to lose weight go on a diet, thereby making what they eat a day long focus!) The simple answer is get a life that you love. Remember as a child your parents worried and tried to ensure you ate something 'else you'll starve to death' yet you were too busy having fun to be bothered by all that eating fuss?

So, after all that ranting: my recipe for curing the world. Don't do sympathy it's not helpful! Instead do compassion, say something like, *"I'm sorry to hear that, would you like to get over that/move on from that/cure that/solve that?"* Then give them the name of an expert in that field and run away quick before they contaminate you with their poison!! Better still be silently compassionate, if you can.

You have to keep yourself fit mentally, emotionally and spiritually as well as physically, in order to be able to lift anyone else out of the morass. Doctors can't afford to get sick. It's not a selfish thing it's a **selfless** thing. How can you fix anyone else if you're broken yourself? How can you lead others out of a mess if you're in a mess of your own? So don't buy into anyone's scepticism or negativity. EVER. It doesn't help anything. EVER.

However, don't believe this hearsay from me, prove this for yourself. By and large the cynical and sceptical society that we live in doesn't believe this. I frequently hear, when people ask me what I do, comments like, *"Oh yeah, the power of positive thought!"* This is sometimes delivered with a barely disguised sneer and often no attempt to disguise it at all.

The point is that it is not the power of positive thought but simply THE POWER OF THOUGHT.

The sceptics will think, *"I will win a million on the lottery tonight."* They may even repeat it like a mantra all day or all night, though probably only a few repetitions. Deep down of course their subconscious doesn't believe it's possible so it's saying *"Yeah, right."*

So you have a lack of integrity which confuses and weakens the power of your thought. The sceptics then say, *"See I knew it wouldn't work."* And they give up. Justifying their negativity and settling for feeling that they were right as compensation for the fact that it didn't work. Bless!

However the real truth is that, AS YOU THINK SO SHALL YOU BE.

Put another way, WHAT YOU FOCUS ON EXPANDS. If you think you are a loser you have more likelihood of losing. If you think of yourself as a winner you will get more of what you are choosing for yourself. YOU WILL GET TO BE RIGHT ABOUT WHAT YOU THINK.

So focus on what you want more of, not what you seek to avoid. If you think the world is a dangerous violent place you will probably watch the news just to scare yourself more. If you think life is fun and full of nice things and people you will spend little time watching the doom and gloom on TV but be out there living life to the full - your life - your choice.

If, as many people in our culture, you have a basically negative mindset it is probably the power of negative thought that is working in your life. You'd like each day to turn out fine but your superior past experience tells you it probably won't. So in effect you are focusing on having a bad day. Hey guess what, you'll probably be right again and again and again. Now pat yourself on the back, give yourself credit for creating a bad day at will and ask yourself the question, 'but why do I want to do that?' Then decide to STOP IT!

Try this experiment. Go for a walk and hold in mind that you would like plenty of people to smile at you. Engage the eyes of everyone you encounter. Be relaxed and be ready to smile back. Start to believe that everyone may smile at you. They might! It's not impossible and now go for that short walk. Walk slowly. Look up, relax and imagine everyone smiling at you. If you have any doubt that they will, let that doubt go.

When you try this experiment with the full and focused intent that everyone will smile at you, you will find that it works, they will. If at first it doesn't work very well it's just because you haven't released all your doubts or fears about it working. So do that now and try it again.

If you were conversely to decide that people won't smile at you, you will probably exude a negative unwelcoming energy and you are likely to dissuade them from doing so even if their nature would be to smile. Although, others have the right to smile at you, even if you choose to be a miserable git! So there.

Try both these experiments and see what you learn.

The key here is to hold nothing else in your mind than the thought of having people smile at you. It's good practice. Use visualisation too. See them in your minds eye. The more you develop this ability the better your sports performances will be. See your desired outcome as though it has already happened.

Concentration

It is difficult and counter productive to try to concentrate on too many things. I will repeat that: It is difficult and counter productive to try to concentrate on too many things.
Stuff often goes wrong. I believe this is a major cause of

stress. People who think they are good multi-taskers are usually not good at it at all. They make too many mistakes ending up having to do tasks again and are very busy but often just not effective. Doing one thing well to completion is a less stressful and more effective way, perhaps not always easy, but **always less stressful** and **always more effective**. An artist is unlikely to effectively create or capture a scene if her mind is on bills that have to be paid or ANY distraction. A javelin thrower will be compromised by worrying whether his laces are tied etc. This isn't rocket science yet few of us are clear about it.

A great teacher of mine is Hale Dwoskin - he has written a wonderful, life changing book called The Sedona Method. He says, to **eradicate stress** and **maximise your effectiveness** *"Do what you're doing when you're doing it and DON'T DO WHAT YOU'RE NOT DOING WHEN YOU'RE NOT DOING IT!"*

I am sure you've seen people who aren't really there fully. Pretty insulting really but self damaging for them too. So they meet you for lunch but mentally and emotionally they're somewhere else. To start with it takes a little effort, a little organising but introduce this ethic into your life:

"Do what you're doing when you're doing it and DON'T DO WHAT YOU'RE NOT DOING WHEN YOU'RE NOT DOING IT!"

By increasing your awareness you can do more concurrently BUT:

NOTHING CUTS THROUGH LIKE PURE UNDILUTED MENTAL FOCUS.

Look at, admire, be inspired by and emulate Jonny Wilkinson. Less obvious to spectators but just as good a role model is Martin Johnson a quiet, calm self belief. If you

74

know you're the best captain of the best Rugby side in the world you don't NEED to tell anyone. Actions speak louder than words, right actions even louder still. Martin Johnson is a giant of a leader, absolutely inspirational. Our politicians could do well to watch and learn. Hollow promises, never enrolling the wishes of the people, simply steamrollering their own vested interest rules and regulations on a misled public! Watch Martin Johnson and learn. A favourite teacher and author of mine is Stuart Wilde.

He once said of politicians, " I don't vote - I don't like to encourage them!"

Oops, I appear to have gone off on one there again!

Anyhow, the point being that a skill to practice is:

CALM, ABSOLUTELY ASSURED, SINGLE POINTED FOCUS, ON A CLEARLY DEFINED DESIRED OUTCOME.

So practice concentration. How do I do that Martyn? Simple, just do it! Practice concentration. Every day. Whatever you're doing. Give it your utmost and undivided attention. Wash the car and see if you can concentrate on it absolutely. Stay in the moment. Don't allow the past to infringe through memories (good or otherwise). Don't allow the future to push its way in. To help, you may repeat silently 'I love washing my car.'

If you wish to relax, find a quiet corner, light a candle and just relaxing your eyes let them settle on the flame and observe the flame for as long as you can. If any thoughts come up let them go and hold the thought, 'I am observing the flame.'

Visualisation

Practice both with your eyes closed and open. Think of something you'd like to achieve. Look in your 'goals and gains' book for a goal. Now see it in your mind's eye as already having been achieved. If you're a football defender you may have a goal:
I love contributing to keeping a clean sheet and I love winning every ball that I go for and going for every ball that is appropriate and in so doing helping my side to win.

So now imagine that. Imagine walking off the pitch. Imagine your goal achieved. Hear the crowd, the mass of the crowd but also the identifiable individual voices ....'well played (insert your name or nickname),' smell the grass, smell any other smell that touches your senses, feel the pleasure of winning, feel the pride and pleasure of delivering a perfect performance, feel the joy you have helped create for the fans, the directors, the coaches and manager and your personal mind coach. (Come on, if you're a really committed professional you will have your own mind coach.)

By practising this visualisation technique you fill up your conscious mind and start to fill your subconscious mind with thoughts of possibility. It makes less room for doubt and negativity.

Years ago, in another lifetime, I was a salesman for a brewery. We were often harangued for a 'deal' and would give a free keg of one of our own products if the landlord would take a sizeable order for Guinness and cider (products that all the other main brewers sold). Basically, if we couldn't sell more of our own products - which were very GOOD! - then we'd fill the cellar up with anything. When the next salesman walked through the door and tried to sell quantities of his products sadly there was no room in the cellar! Shame.

Old trick, simple trick and effectively that's what you're doing with your mind here. Fill it up with possibilities and there's less room for doubts and thoughts that simply don't serve you.

Old trick BUT IT WORKS!

Here's a thing. Visualising gives you a double whammy. By imagining how well something could turn out you are giving yourself a mental and emotional rehearsal so you'll be better prepared when life hands you what you're looking for.

Yet also it may help to bring deeply buried doubt or negative and destructive beliefs, to the surface. You can then just decide to let them go and practice your new found skill of letting go of baggage that doesn't help or serve you. Brilliant! Many people experience this. They start to visualise their dreams. Up comes some doubt and they give in to it. They believe it. But often our thoughts, beliefs and feelings just lie. Just because you doubt your ability to do something doesn't mean you can't. It just means you have some doubt that you can. That's all! Rather than arguing with doubt say, 'okay but what if WERE possible?' That usually shuts it up.

AFTER ALL IF YOU HAD NO DOUBT ABOUT YOUR ABILITIES WHERE WOULD THE CHALLENGE OR FUN BE?

Everybody could be the best in the world there'd be nothing special about it if not for the challenge of overcoming doubt.

In her brilliant book Feel The Fear and Do it Anyway author Susan Jeffers shows us that courage is not the absence of fear but looking your fear in the face and overcoming it. That's courage. So too self belief is not the absence of doubt but the product of having the courage to overcome doubt. Back to that old chestnut - you've got to acknowledge it, look at it to win over it. And that's the joy!

Back to visualisation, I've been very lucky to work with a fine young cricketer. Steve Kirby of Yorkshire and England A. He's a very talented quick bowler. I am absolutely certain that when he gets his chance he will become an England great. I am privileged because he's a top bloke but also because he has honed his visualisation skills massively. He has to be one of the best. I'd love to sit with Jonny Wilkinson and Kirbs and see if between us we could take the tool to a new level. I believe there is no limit. It would certainly be fun seeing where it is if there is one! These guys are masters and it shows.

I am sure that when David Beckham stepped up to kick England into the world cup with his equalising last minute free kick against Greece his self belief in that moment was **beyond belief**. This was his destiny. He KNEW he was going to score. WE KNEW he was going to score! THEY KNEW he was going to score. These brilliant sports performers are, at times, tapping into the superconscious and they can SEE and FEEL the result of their endeavour even before it has happened. Their challenge is to engage the superconscious more frequently or even constantly and they do.

So, CONCENTRATION - single pointed focus - and VISU-ALISATION are massive tools for opening to greater possibility and bringing to the surface deep seated and hidden subconscious thoughts, feelings and beliefs that hold you back. They also, the more you practice them, help to engage the superconscious. Then the unexplainable starts to happen. Don't ask me to explain! You begin to manage your coincidences. You begin to create your own luck. You stop believing in coincidences. You stop believing in luck. You start becoming very grateful that you found this tool! You simplify. You stop worrying because you know that is focusing on a result you don't want. You acknowledge your concern, thank it for the warning it brings, then let it go and refocus on your desired outcome and go for it with courage.

SO YOU'VE SET YOUR GOAL. YOU'RE STRENGTHEN-ING YOUR ABILITY TO FOCUS, LET'S NOW LOOK AT REMOVING THE LAST TRACES OF NEGATIVITY.

7 Eradicating negativity

"Confidence is a strange phenomenon." - **Bob Woolmer**

The reason we wish to eradicate negativity is so that when we practice our powerful, single pointed focus on our desired goal, that focus is not diluted with other thoughts. **Any negative thought is expressing a desire for that negative outcome to become real.** We all know that what we focus on expands, so to focus on something that you don't want to happen is just dopey, you may be aware of the danger but you don't need to focus on it.

It's mad! Why would you do that? You now KNOW from experimenting yourself that negative thoughts lead to negative outcomes. You may naturally have them arise in your consciousness but you don't have to give them power by holding on to them.

Simply observe the negative thought, thank it for the warning it brings and let it go. You don't want it, you don't need it for later. It's done its job in warning you. An example is some feelings that you may not win in a given situation. Great. Job done. I have been warned not to be complacent now I can switch my focus to the process of doing what I'm doing to the best of my ability and if I take care of what I can take care of, then the result will take care of itself. Thanks.

So get into the habit of spotting the tendency to blame, to complain, to judge (as opposed to observe) and practice your now growing ability to let these negative, fear-based bad habits go. See if you can go for an hour without having any negative thoughts. Sometimes you will, sometimes you won't, but keep releasing anything negative and hold in mind something positive and you will get there. One day you'll think 'ooh I must remember to drop negative thoughts today' and you'll realise that you actually can't remember the last time you had one.

A good trick is to hold in mind this question, what if, even though I don't understand why, everything is turning out perfectly? The rational mind wants to argue with the question. It's okay, that's what it does. But what if, just WHAT IF everything is turning out perfectly? It's just that you can't see how. Could you trust that it is? Try it.

Polarity releasing

Here's another method of releasing negative thoughts and feelings. Remember thoughts are just thoughts, they are not who we are - although many people choose to identify heavily with them - and as such you can let them go. And remember too that feelings are just feelings and they too can be released.

People say things like, *"look at that angry person"* or *"she's a very sad woman."* Of course this is misleading, no one is really sad or angry they are just displaying those emotions because they are holding on to them, probably stuck in them. Of course YOU are learning that that is just a choice. An unconscious choice by them maybe, but a choice nevertheless. Once you know it is a choice you can choose to stay stuck or you can choose little by little (or lot by lot) to let go of these emotions, that are helping no one, by you holding on. Your state is just a state. It's not who you are. And YOU choose your state. Happiness is not a mood. Well it is but it's also simply a decision or a choice. It is.

So here's the other method. As I mentioned before, we live in a world of duality or polarities - you can't have anything without its opposite. You can't have good without bad - HOW WOULD YOU KNOW WHAT IT WAS!!!
You can't have happy without sad - HOW WOULD YOU KNOW THAT YOU WERE HAPPY!!

Yet we try to live our lives as though we can have all of one and not the other. So we try to block out the bad by suppressing it and thereby holding on to it in our subconscious mind.

WHY?????

IT'S MAD!!!!!!

JUST LET IT GO!!!

Here's another way to release stuck thoughts or feelings. We are stuck because we are resisting the inherent duality. So we simply switch between the polarities (or duality extremes) and you will feel them dissolve until they just don't matter anymore and then they naturally release and are gone for good. So let's start with self belief. Ask yourself this pair of questions and, taking your time, just switch from one to the other remembering to answer. You can answer yes or no it doesn't matter which but do answer honestly otherwise you will struggle to change anything for the better.

Can you acknowledge that you may have some doubt about your ability somewhere in your being?
...don't forget to answer

And now can you let go of doubt and be open to growing massive self belief as best you can?   Answer?

Again,
Can you acknowledge that you may have some doubt about your ability somewhere in your being?
(this may be your subconscious)
...don't forget to answer

And now can you let go of doubt and be open to growing massive self belief?   Answer?

Again,
Can you acknowledge that you may have had some doubt about your ability in the past?
...don't forget to answer

Now can you let go of doubt and allow yourself to grow massive self belief as best you can?   Answer?

Again,
Can you acknowledge that you may have had some doubt about your ability in the past?
...don't forget to answer

Now let go of doubt and allow yourself to easily grow massive self belief?   Answer?

You should notice a change. It may be that you were resisting admitting (denying), to start with, that you have any doubt or the thought that you could have massive self belief seemed unlikely.

It doesn't matter but as you switch between the pairings the feelings will soften.

It may be that you will get a big energy shift, many people do, there is a lot of stored up negative energy and when it releases it can feel like a big weight off your shoulders. Sometimes a big sigh of relief or a deep breath happens involuntarily.

Personally when I get a shift or release of energy it starts me sneezing, some people yawn. All of it is OK. It's suppressed negative energy being released. You might feel slightly emotional, that's OK too. Suddenly it won't feel such an issue and eventually you will feel lighter about it.

It may be that you don't feel much at all but continue to ask yourself the questions. You may only notice the effects when you realise that you are more relaxed during your performance, at times when you would have been tense in the past. This will obviously manifest in your performance standard being higher and you enjoying it more. That can snowball infinitely.

Now here's some more suggested polarities, then you can try making up your own.

Can I acknowledge that sometimes I distrust my ability / technique / reactions / strength etc.?

> *Don't forget to answer yourself.*

And now can I let go of distrust and trust myself more with every breath I take?

> *Answer please!*

Can I acknowledge that sometimes I think I may not be good enough?   Yes / No
And now can I let go of those thoughts and be open to the possibility that I can easily be good enough?   Yes / No

Can I acknowledge that I may feel that I cannot improve further?   Yes / No
And now can I let go of that thought and allow myself to enjoy improving?   Yes / No

Can I acknowledge that I think there are limits to how good I could be?   Yes / No
Now can I let go of any concept of limits and simply enjoy exploring how good I could be?   Yes / No

Remember to keep switching between the two and ANSWERING. I highly recommend practising this. Don't just read and understand. Do it. Don't believe it works. HAVE it working more and more for you in your life.

Be aware of your thoughts and feelings. Don't get over analytical just see if they are positive or negative, see if they lift you or drag you down. Then what? Well, if you have a negative thought simply turn it to a positive one.

If you catch yourself hoping things won't (neg) go wrong (neg) then drop that thought and hope that things will (pos) go right (pos).

If you catch yourself thinking, 'I bet I'm going to be late (neg)' instead think, 'I choose to be on time (pos).'

AT THE RISK OF REPEATING MYSELF - HOW THE HELL ARE YOU GOING TO GET WHAT YOU CHOOSE IF YOU ARE ALWAYS FOCUSED ON WHAT YOU DON'T WANT???

So choose positive attitudes. They will help you drag yourself out of the negativity of your past and that of others. Mother Theresa was once asked if she would march against war. She said, "No, but if you have a march FOR peace, I'll be there."

Don't contaminate your own power with negativity OR (better) empower yourself with positivity.
EMPOWER YOURSELF WITH POSITIVITY.

Being grateful and gracious

It is very hard to have an external attitude that is different to your internal one. In fact it may just be impossible. And of course it doesn't fool anyone. It never looks sincere.

In the midst of Australia's cricket near whitewash of England in Australia 2002/2003, the England captain Nasser Hussain stated 'there is no psychological advantage that Australia have, we just need to work harder on our technique.'

England were 3-0 down at the time and lost 4-1. Whilst this was a brave attempt to look as though the tourists had a modicum of self belief it was not well thought out. Had he said that England's self belief was shot to pieces, that psychologically the Aussies had a massive advantage and that England were going to do the best they could to rebuild, then he may have had a little more success. (The Australians may have been lulled into a false sense of security and dropped their level of performance, although I doubt it, but more importantly they would have taken Hussain's comments as arrogance - and wanted to punish him and the England team MORE). Surely the point of saying anything in such a situation is to motivate your own troops not the opposition!

Now I'm not attacking Nasser because he didn't know any better. But if England wish to win the next cricket World Cup then up to date software for the mind (like PP) might be better than the 70 year old technology that Freudian psychoanalysis is. That is what is currently practised by most sports psychologists.

I AM PREPARED TO STICK MY NECK OUT NOW AND PREDICT THAT THE NEXT WORLD CUP WILL BE WON BY THE NATION THAT HAS THE BEST MIND COACH. Ok - so I'm biased!!

Obviously, everybody watching Nasser's interview could see that he didn't believe, himself, what he was saying. He may even have lost some respect as captain from his team too. If you had the same self belief as your opponents then no psychological advantage would exist but you wouldn't be 3-0 down and you WOULDN'T be talking about a need to work harder on technique! That implies quite clearly that you don't believe you're good enough.

The rest of the world could see that Nasser was in a massive denial of the reality of the situation. Perhaps he's a sceptic and doesn't believe in what he can't see. However, sadly for him, the fact that you don't believe in something doesn't mean it doesn't exist! This is called delusion. It is exactly the same with someone who everyone can see is an alcoholic. They say they don't have a drink problem, everyone else can see that they do. The problem for any one stuck in denial is that they can't cure the problem. As Nasser couldn't cure the problem of the Aussies supremacy because he wouldn't or couldn't see the nature of it. You see at that level they can all play. **Form is a direct result of self belief.** Some people believe in luck but what if that's just an excuse? What if that belief makes you a victim of your circumstances? - sometimes you're in form, sometimes you're not - well in my experience and research that's simply not true!

Gary Player said, *"The harder I work, the luckier I get."*
Top performers in ALL fields of human existence now know that hard work needs to not just be haphazard but **focused right action**, not just physical but **holistic**, i.e. across the whole of our experience - therefore balancing physical, mental, emotional and spiritual effort to gain the highest quality of result.

Conversely to the Australia v England contest above, contrast the England Rugby World Cup win in Australia in November 2003. Clive Woodward clearly is a man who knows the value of psychology. Sometimes called the science of success it is simply the gaining knowledge of how we as humans work BEST. What is there to be scared of?
Clive Woodward develops his player's mindset as well as all other areas of their preparation that he sees as key to the

success. The Australians, South Africans, French, New Zealanders will all be dissecting Woodward's approach to beat him in 2007. No room for arrogance they will be grateful that he has lifted the game to a new level. They will graciously accept (not necessarily like) his success and use it to motivate themselves to higher levels of achievement. **Grace and gratitude** - positive and powerful tools in achieving your highest success.

Developing self trust

It's not a question, in our society that we ask very often, *"Do I trust myself."* We tend to focus on others and distrust or trust others. However, you do see sports performers trusting themselves much more than the man in the street. You will hear players say that they back themselves. The man in the street typically has a victim mentality, *"It'll probably go wrong and if it does go right, I'll probably get taxed on it."* It is clear, that if you trust yourself or trust your godgiven talent then you'll have less internal or infernal interference in your performances. You'll not need to try as hard, you'll be more relaxed, you'll still be focused - more so because your doubts will be less and less as time goes on.

So, could you see yourself performing with absolute self belief, with the total absence of doubt? Could you trust yourself to hold that state throughout a whole performance? Could you trust yourself to hold that state under extreme pressure of competition?

If you could, good. But for the mere mortals amongst us and for the moments of doubt in the immortals amongst you out there (you might be on your own Jonny), here's another exercise.

Could you acknowledge that you may sometimes distrust your ability?   Yes/No
Now can you let that go and allow yourself to trust your-

self as best you can?   Yes/No
(repeat this several times and remember to answer each
question and really let go)

Could you acknowledge that you may distrust life to work
out the way you hoped or planned?   Yes/No
And now can you let go of distrust and consider what if,
just what if, everything is turning out perfectly?   Yes/No

Can I acknowledge that I sometimes distrust myself?
Now can I relax and trust myself absolutely, just as best I
can?

I breathe out distrust.
I breathe in deep unshakeable self trust.

What if, just what if, absolute self belief is possible?

8 Getting into 'The Zone'

"Hey Johnny, what is va va voom?" - **Thierry Henry**

No one knows what va va voom is and very few know what 'The Zone' is. It is where genius exists.

Many people have experienced this 'zone of optimum performance', more haven't.

Earlier I described David Lloyd's experience. When I interviewed Paul Allott the former Lancashire and England seam bowler he talked about a similar state. He didn't need to think about what he wanted to do. He just knew, he just ran in and it all seemed to work like clock work. Almost as if he wasn't doing it, he was just witnessing it. Others report time being flexible, everything seeming to happen in slow motion. Some of my clients have described the ball as having 'sat up and waited to be hit.' How often do you hear, "He must be seeing it like a football."

Until now those who have, have mostly felt it was bestowed upon them. In a way, it is. Yet we can encourage the phenomenon to occur by practising right action.

To recap, those actions are:

Having a clear outcome in a clear, quiet mind, i.e. no doubts or negativity (either in your conscious mind or subconscious mind - often suppressed there through denial.)

Being open to limitless possibility.

Being positive, gracious, grateful, calm and physically relaxed. (From this state if you then want to pretend to be aggressive to upset your opponent's concentration then you can pretend.)

Having absolute focus (on what you choose, not what you don't choose.)

Being able to constantly and quickly deal with any negative emotion, thought or habitual belief. Not by suppressing or expressing but by letting go or releasing. (For more specific help on this subject visit: www.martyncourt.co.uk and look for Sedona Method.)

Finally, to really encourage this state of 'the zone' to be bestowed upon you, you need to drop your ego.

You need to move away from the sense that it's all about you. You can't be the greatest; golfer, bowler, batsman, tennis player, scrum half, fly half, entertainer, boxer, centre forward, whatever ON YOUR OWN. Who wants to be the best in a field of one? You need others, including tough opposition, if you are going to be able to show your talent. You may not want them but you need them. Did you ever see, as a kid, the boy with the new football? Everyone joins in, they're better than him, he can't get a kick. So he gets frustrated, picks up the ball and says it's his ball and they can't play with it. They say, "uuuhhuu" and wander off. His victory is bitter sweet. He has his ball but a game with a ball but no team members is dull, with no opposition, not much of a challenge. Doh!

So think of yourself as a pawn in the game (even in the game of life) simply trying to be a good pawn. That will help you be less of a pain in the arse to live with and will help you drop your ego. Martin Johnson is awesome in this regard. On the pitch, an opponent can punch him in the face. He doesn't get involved. His little ego (honour or any such sense of self importance) doesn't need protecting. He has a more important cause to pursue - the discipline that will help him and his team to win again - so he smiles.

You see when you drop your ego (many mistake this for

confidence or self belief - it isn't, that is calm and quiet - but it's a symptom of arrogance and comes from insecurity and lack of self belief). When you drop your ego you invoke the superconscious. The superconscious is also known as spirit. Now spirit means different things to different people. A drinker thinks of Jack Daniels and coke or Bombay Sapphire and tonic or meths. A religious person thinks of something different. Here, however, I mean the essence of you as a human being. Or as the spirit of a game means the fundamental essence of that game. The ancient Greeks originated our word enthusiasm from their phrase 'En theos' meaning with spirit. So when you absolutely love something and you do it with enthusiasm and spirit, you then stand the best chance of invoking 'the zone'. When you do, even for a fleeting moment, acknowledge it to yourself.

Be grateful as though you have been specially blessed. You have. And just as any of us give more to those who appreciate our gifts, you too will be granted more of the 'Zone'.

Thankyou for staying with me this far. If you have enjoyed this read please tell your friends and team mates. Not your opponents obviously! And if you didn't enjoy this at all - shut up about it already, I've heard enough!!

And for the cynics.

Yes I know you've heard it all before. I only said it was new and powerful (it IS powerful) because the marketing men told me to so we could sell some copies. I know it's not new. Nothing is. It's all been said before. But not by me and not now, exactly like this, so there!

One more thing - a word about cynics. It comes from a Greek word for dog. The cynics were renowned for their anger and hatred of society which they displayed by urinating publicly in the street gaining the name dog-men. So now you know what a cynic is, you can smile compassionately and leave them to their self imposed misery. Of course they call it realism. Bless!

9 The Yips

"Defeat is worse than death. You have to live with defeat."
- **Bill Shankly**

When David Lloyd and others described to me their experience of being in the 'Zone' they clearly described a thought free state. For some this experience of the 'Zone' or being run by the subconscious is more mundane. You have been driving for some time then become conscious that you don't really remember the last ten miles. You've been in a 'Zone' and operating on auto pilot. It is similar but your conscious mind has probably been fairly active, just occupied on some other area of concern.

However, the 'Zone' is a thought free state. You know, or decide what you want to do, then just do it with total clarity. No need for thought, it just gets in the way!

Taken to the extreme too much thought can paralyse you. If you are a golfer faced with a putt, you have the thought that you wish to sink the putt, this becomes a decision to do exactly that and without further thought but single pointed focus you hit the putt firmly and purposefully and sink it. However, if there is an element of difficulty to the putt or if indeed hundreds of thousands of whatever your currency is, is at stake, then your fear based rational mind starts to think of the ways in which it could go wrong. You're not far from mental overwhelm and indecision. Very far from the thought free state. This mental overwhelm can become severe enough to paralyse the player and sometimes results in involuntary movements. I have heard of cases where golfers have been carried from the course frozen in their back swing. This has been called the 'Yips'.

I was fortunate enough to work with cricketer Gavin Hamilton. Gavin had a successful World Cup campaign in 1999 with Scotland followed by an England Test call up.

Shortly afterwards though, Gavin suffered the Yips. After bowling five wides in his first over he asked to be taken out of the attack and then struggled to recover his confidence to bowl for the next two years. During that time many conventional sport psychologists and others including Paul Mckenna tried to help, with no apparent success.

Toward the end of summer 2003 Gavin and I met. We exchanged niceties and did some subconscious clean up work. Much of the concepts were new to Gavin but he had been looking into understanding why it had all gone wrong so he was quite open.

I suggested that we cut to the chase. How about letting go of wanting to understand the problem? How about let's just fix it?

That weekend Gavin went to bowl for his club in the Bradford League and took 4 wickets. He had two games for Yorkshire 2's. before the end of the season where he returned 2 for 20 style figures. Yorkshire decided at the end of the season to let him go.

Having moved to Durham where Martyn Moxon is a very supportive and intuitive coach, Gavin and I continued to clean his subconscious mind of the negativity that Gavin had tried hard to ignore. His first First Class wickets for two years came against Durham UCCE - four wickets to be precise.

More significant was the 22 overs that Gav bowled against Nottinghamshire in April. First innings figures of 6 overs 0 wickets for 14 runs looks tidy but in the second innings a bulkier contribution was 22 overs 1 wicket for 99 runs. This doesn't look great but 20 runs were taken off the last over before lunch. Having had all lunch time to brood over it and the choice of not bowling further in the match Gavin had the strength to take the ball after lunch and carry on. THAT was significant! Later a thumb ligament injury ruled

Gavin out for some weeks. There is no doubt in my mind that Gavin has successfully laid the ghosts that have haunted him and now knows that he has the mental strength to deal with the Yips should anything reoccur.

Also it is significant, as I now know that these tools that I have developed, WORK. Paraconscious Programming™ succeeds where many other psychological methods have failed. There is hope for the most extreme performance 'wobbles'. **MOREOVER this is a method that can take performers beyond the levels that they may consciously believe are possible, to higher levels of performance than have ever been achieved before.**

10 Case Studies

"Physical toughness will make the opponent weaken, mental toughnes will make him crack." - **Vince Lombardi**

During the past few years, in the process of developing Paraconscious Programming™, I have worked in various situations and with a wide range of performers. These are some of the cases which I believe point to the scope and unlimited potential of Paraconscious Programming™.

Damian Brandy, Leicestershire CCC

At the back end of summer 2002, Leicester's head coach Phil Whitticase said to me, 'If you can help Damo it will prove the power of your method.' Damian had scored freely as a youth player but on securing a senior contract had become stuck on 35. He always looked full of ability but seemed to have a mental block and would frequently get out around 35.

I was introduced to Leicestershire 2nd XI and spent a 3 day game getting to know the coach and players. Well, more just being around, allowing acclimatisation to take place. I watched Damian bat beautifully until, in the 30s, he contrived to get himself out. Sometime the following week Damo approached me to do some work together. We just sat in the empty stand at Grace Road (Leicestershire's home ground) and spent around an hour and a half in small talk until Damian was comfortable, then about 30 minutes actually using the Paraconscious Programming ™ techniques. He probably didn't sense the difference. I was able to help him change his subconscious mindset, particularly hidden resentments and wrong focus. Damo had come to focus on what he didn't want in certain areas and was inhibiting his natural flair. Just by getting him to ask himself certain questions, using some polarity releasing, I was able to gently help him change his perspective. A perspective he didn't know he had acquired! This process is subconscious so, often, the subject only feels as though we are having a 'chat'. Much 'sports psychology' is simply Freudian psycho-analysis. I'm not knocking it but it is 70 year old technology and can often seem intrusive, telling the subject what they already know. It offers analysis and understanding but often no simple, effective and rapid cure.

After our chat Damian probably felt very little change but in his next game he scored 60-odd in each innings, an 80 in the next game, 90-odd in the next, then 147 v. Warwickshire 2's. His next game was his 1st XI debut v. Somerset in a day/night game where he made a very bright 35! So the results of our working together were enormously powerful and immediate.

Cheltenham Town Football Club

When Bobby Gould invited me in to work with him and the players at Cheltenham time was running out. Bobby had taken over from Graham Allner and had 20 games left of the season to earn Cheltenham another term in Division Two and himself a more permanent job. His 8 games in charge (before I joined) had yielded 1 win 3 draws and 4 defeats. The last, against Bristol City and a 3-1 defeat, I observed from the bench and dressing room.

Steve Cotterill had been the manager that had taken Cheltenham from non-league status to Division Two but left for Stoke City, leaving behind the clear impression that he thought the players weren't good enough to stay in Division Two. The players had bought it. The club had spent the entire season in the bottom four relegation zone but had now gone bottom and drifted away from the pack for the first time.

On Monday morning I started work. There was a clear ring leader but in general the mindset was negative anyway. With the loss of Cotterill most of the players self belief had left too. Talk was of next year's cut in wages (after relegation) and generally of financial down-sizing doom and gloom. This was fuelled by a negative ring leader, that many looked up to, and a bus driver who had he been any more negative or cynical would have disappeared up his own vortex! He justified this as realism!

Bobby Gould was courageous in introducing me and encouraged everyone to be open to my work. Some were, others less so. The immediate challenge for me was to change the team mindset from the negative, apathetic one I found to one that could consider the possibility that we could actually win games and get out of this. The majority of players took on my concepts and were open to the work immediately. The belief existed that bad luck would befall the side but no good fortune, bad refereeing decisions but no good ones. We had become unlucky so what was the point of giving your best? Certain players had personal issues and gripes against the club or whatever and were simply failing to produce their best. The 'zone' is a thought free state.

Most of these players had more issues than a newsagent. On the team bus to our first game since my involvement I was worried. There were two distinct groups; a group of about four players who I had spent time with were playing cards, relaxed, light easy laughter characterised them. The rest were sniping, moody, tense and negative sarcasm characterised them. I thought we couldn't win. We got lucky, the pitch was water logged, the ref called it off, we went home. This gave me a little more time.

During the week I picked key players and worked at gaining a core of players who I would reprogram to be right thinking and positive and open to possibility. We included the possibility that at some stage before the end of the season we would be lucky enough to get a penalty and that we could score 4 goals in a game and that we actually had played most sides off the park for periods so we could beat

most sides in the division. We just needed to go and do it. Of course anyone can say this stuff I had to have the players believe it in their subconscious mind. That is my challenge. It worked. We beat Mansfield 3-1. We had a genuine foul in the penalty area given and we scored our first penalty of the season. AND after the game John Brough came off the pitch and punched me on the arm, " We got the 4 goals!" He shouted in my face with delight, a clenched fist in the air and one on my arm. I still have the bruise. Although we had won only 3-1 we had actually scored a legitimate goal from a corner. The keeper, under no pressure or contact missed claiming the corner. He fell to the floor, probably in embarrassment. Jamie Victory, unchallenged, headed into an empty net but the referee gave them a free kick. The video showed clearly that the goal should have stood. We didn't care 3-1 was good enough, we were on our way to a recovery.

Tuesday we played the postponed fixture at Swindon, won 3-0 and were off the bottom. The next game was at home against Northampton. A win would get us out of the bottom four for the first time all year. When you are building self belief there is a pinnacle at which the challenge is to 'hold it there'. To not go over into complacency - a form of arrogance, the pride that comes before a fall. Bobby and I discussed this and I went away to consider how best to avoid that trap. I had been doing a subconscious clean up before games and sometimes even the team talk before kick off, just to ensure everyone's focus was where it should be. Sadly on this occasion I didn't do the pre-match chat and so the need to avoid COMPLACENCY was the
theme. Constantly reinforcing that COMPLACENCY was to be avoided at all cost, that we really must watch for COMPLACENCY creeping in. No one was to be COMPLA-CENT!!
It took 70 minutes for the deadlock to be broken in a tense derby relegation battle. Mark Yates, the captain, popped up with what could be the winner. We had not won three on

the trot all year and this would take us out of the bottom four. 10 minutes to go and the COMPLACENCY crept in. Just for a moment we relaxed mentally, the back four dropped off and suddenly we are defending on the edge of our box. We are letting them push onto us which we hadn't done all game. They equalise. Two valuable points gone. We're still in the bottom four. And we got what we focused on - COMPLACENCY.

The season from there remained tantalisingly alive. Bobby Gould and his assistant got new contracts many of the players played to their best form and the crowds grew steadily from the low 3400 before I became involved. It all came down to the last game where we travelled to Notts. County needing to win to stay up. We enjoyed a record travelling crowd. If we won, County's near rivals Chesterfield would go down. It looked like they had this in mind. Bobby Gould's position was now safe and he must have decided to lose the game to make next season easier, or so he could come up in a blaze of glory as Division Three Champions. There could be no other explanation for what he did next. He changed a successful team around with several changes, playing central defender Mike Duff out of position. Not just up front as a target man/centre forward but as a left winger. He'd never played there before. A player who Gould had berated as useless and put on the transfer list, and had not been able to hold a place down, was played in place of the player who had held that position and was fit to play etc. All the pre-match routines we had developed were cast aside. The manager stood outside the dugout, rather than in his usual spot. He told the assistant manager to be quiet and to sit down when he got up to urge the players on. At half time 1-0 down he demanded silence in the dressing room and when the captain tried to rally everyone he quietened him. It was all slightly surreal. We lost 1-0. We went down to Division Three. I can't help but think it was exactly what Bobby wanted. There can be no other explanation.

My time at the club ended there. The fans gained Bobby Gould's resignation after only a handful of poor performances at the start of the next season. Sadly for him, you reap what you sow.

In the 12 games that I was able to have an effect I helped the gates rise by helping players have the courage to play and express themselves. Not all of them, but enough. I was able to refocus players minds and change simple wrong thinking to right thinking. I was able to teach some players a far more powerful goal setting model and help them stay focused on what they were trying to achieve.
THE RESULTS SPOKE FOR THEMSELVES:

Bobby Gould, before I joined...   Won 1 Drew 3 Lost 4
After I joined...   Won 4 Drew 6 Lost 2

Steve Adshead

I met Steve when I was working with Leicestershire 2nd XI. He had been a pro cricketer for three years always playing for the 2's. He had never been given a chance to prove himself in the first team. This lead to an increase in frustration, increasing anger and resentment. He was released from Leicestershire his career potentially ended.
I received a phone call from him, " Right what's all this positive thinking rubbish? If you're any good come and help me."

Steve hadn't really been this low before but he had the courage to seek help. Many never do. I taught him to process and release deep seated anger and loss of self belief. We worked massively on self belief. He matured rapidly. He really took it all on board and was quick to learn these tools. His ability to focus and concentrate were highly tuned but he was able to learn quickly and spent the next season playing minor county cricket and as a non contract player for counties all around the country. He impressed wherever he went, he scored masses of runs wherever he went. He played for Leicestershire (again), Somerset, Gloucestershire, Worcestershire, Shropshire and other representative sides. He was enjoying his cricket and playing some of the best cricket of his life. We worked on him learning what he needed to put himself in the 'zone' and he became better at it.

Steve has now succeeded the legendary Jack Russell at Gloucestershire. He can't replace Jack, Jack is unique but Steve takes stumpings stood up to the pace bowlers in one day games, as Jack pioneered, and scores runs. It's early days yet but if England are to find a cricketer nearer to Adam Gilchrist's standards, then this just might be the man.

Lloyd Tennant

Lloyd is second team coach at Leicestershire County Cricket Club. As a 17 year old he progressed quickly and toured Sri Lanka with England's young cricketers. He was quick and swung it out. Then came the Yips. "I couldn't be certain that I'd hit the cut strip." Lloyd told me. The coaches at Leicestershire couldn't help him and a move to Essex CCC didn't improve matters either. The coaches changed his natural action to one that has tended to injure his hamstrings with regularity. He dropped out of professional cricket but continued to bowl in the Birmingham league. He hated it, always bowling with the fear that it would go wrong. He would usually bowl the first few overs 'across the seam' so the ball wouldn't swing. He was bowling so far within himself that it didn't feel like bowling properly at all. The fun had gone.

Since Lloyd and I have worked on his subconscious mind he reports feeling calm when bowling (an alien feeling for him). He knows that he is bowling better and better. "Every now and then it comes out really well," he concedes (not one to readily blow his trumpet) and from time to time his natural action returns. He feels quite good about it. Some of the Leicestershire batsman have commented during practice sessions, "Lloyd was sharp this morning." or " Lloyd was quick and shaped it (swung the ball away)."

There's more to come, Lloyd now has some goals to achieve and some he has already achieved. As with all of us it's not the sky that's the limit it's what we think we can or can't achieve that's the limit.

Other Cases

I have worked with many cases whilst developing the methods that I call Paraconscious Programming™ or PP, here briefly are some other gains. So many people think that you only need a mentor or mind specialist when something is wrong. But what constitutes the concept of wrong? Wrong, surely, is only something you don't want. So, are you satisfied with your level of achievement or would you like to surpass what you have already achieved? Or indeed would you like to set new standards? Would you like to go beyond what your conscious mind thinks is possible or reasonable?
It can be done.

I worked with a club cricketer from Dumbleton in Gloucestershire.

Gibbo had been a county second team player and prided himself on his catching and worked hard at it. He and I did a catching drill from a marked starting point. I hit catches off a bat and Gibbo just had to mark on the ground when he took a catch at the limit of his ability on either hand. We didn't measure it. Gibbo marked his range with his studs. He was absolutely convinced (in his conscious mind) that this was the physical limit to his catching ability. ABSOLUTELY CONVINCED. I cleaned his subconscious mind of concepts of limitation and we set off again with the catching drill. Within, say, a dozen catches he took off, held a catch and landed staring at the mark he had made. His hand and the ball were 18 inches beyond his previous best - his conscious limit.

Gibbo leapt to his feet, dropped the ball and stared at his hand in disbelief saying, "**** me Martyn that's scary!" This had all taken about 5-7 minutes.

At the same club I worked with Tom Green, a handy young cricketer who had played County under 17. We did a similar drill to even up a distrust on his left side. He consistently caught 2 foot further on his right side than his left. This was a subconscious distrust of what he had come to think of as his weaker left hand. In about 3 minutes we had evened them up and increased his range by two foot on both hands. All the best county coaching and drills had failed to achieve this.

Tom had, when batting, been playing over the top of square cuts. The shot was right but the execution wrong. Conventional coaching would be to point out the fault and try differing methods of correction. This often takes time. Mark Scott former Worcestershire opening bat and latterly coach assured me that it takes at least 35,000 hits to change a shot. He claimed that he was working with Steve Rhodes to change a shot and it would take weeks.

Well fine, that may be true of conventional coaching.

It most definitely is not true of my methods!

With Tom, in a matter of 5-10 minutes the problem was sorted. I never suggested a fault on which to concentrate or a cure which would also emphasise the fault but through subconscious suggestion and kinaesthetic awareness Tom's body and subconscious mind sorted the problem and he began, and continues, to execute the shot with perfection, consistently.

This has been around for a long time, it always has been true and it always will be true.

> If you think you're beaten, you are.
> If you think you dare not, you don't.
> If you'd like to win, but you think you can't,
> It is almost certain you won't.
>
> If you think you'll lose, you're lost
> For in this world you'll find,
> Success begins with a fellow's will -
> It's all in the state of mind.
>
> If you think you're outclassed, you are,
> You've got to think high to rise,
> You have to be sure of yourself before
> You can ever win a prize.
>
> Life's battles don't always go
> To the stronger or faster man,
> But soon or late, the man who wins
> Is the man who thinks he can!

If you've had the commitment to read this far then thank-you. Now take it one step further and reread, underlining relevant passages and marking pages where exercises are printed.

DO THE EXERCISES.
Then do them again. They will embed in your subconscious and you will program your own mind to be more powerful. You WILL have greater mental strength. You WILL achieve more of what you want. If the little voice said, "Yeah, RIGHT" to any of that then go to page 30 and do the exercises on releasing doubt NOW. You owe it to yourself to have everything in your life the way you would like it (without infringing on others' rights). Inspire yourself, be an inspiration to others by being the best you can be.

Be courageous, step out of your comfort zone and aim higher.

I wish you ALL the VERY best.

Suggested Further Reading

There are many titles to explore but these few I would like to recommend because they are personal favourites. I would like to think that these publications will help to expand your awareness, open your mind and help you to become the best that you can be. Enjoy!

The 7 habits of highly effective people	*Steven Covey* Simon & Schuster 1969
The Power of Now	*Ekhart Tolle*, Hodder & Stoughton 1999
The 10-minute Life Coach	*Fiona Harrold*, Hodder & Stoughton 2002
The Inner Game of Tennis	*Timothy Gallwey* Pan 1974
Losing my virginity	*Richard Branson* Virgin publishing 1998
Mind Store	*Jack Black,* Audio tape Thorsons Audio
It's Not About the Bike	*Lance Armstrong* Yellow Jersey Pr 2001
The Success Coach	*Martyn Court* Sidney Publishing 2002 (www.martyncourt.co.uk)
Creative Visualisation	*Ronald Shone* Thorsons 1984
Silent Power	*Stuart Wilde* Hay House, 1996
Focused for Soccer	*Bill Beswick* 2001
The Warrior Athlete	*Dan Millman*, Stillpoint publishing 1979

The Sedona Method	*Hale Dwoskin* 2003
Golf for Enlightenment	*Deepak Chopra* Rider 2003
Think and Grow Rich	*Napoleon Hill* Frederick Fell Publishing 2002
Opening Up	*Mike Atherton* Coronet 2003
Body Mind Mastery	*Dan Millman* New World 1999
Change Your Life in 7 Days	*Paul McKenna* Bantam Press 2004

ISBN 141202966-X